A DISCOVERY GUIDE

UNDERSEA WORLD

A DISCOVERY GUIDE

UNDERSEA WORLD

DR · RICHARD · PAGETT

a Salamander book

Published by Salamander Books Limited
LONDON • NEW YORK

A Salamander Book

Published by Salamander Books Ltd,
129–137 York Way,
London N7 9LG,
United Kingdom.

ISBN 0 86101 496 0

Distributed in the United Kingdom by
Hodder & Stoughton Services,
PO Box 6, Mill Road,
Dunton Green, Sevenoaks,
Kent TN13 2XX.

Editor: Mark Bathurst
Designer: Rod Ferring
Colour artwork: © Salamander Books Ltd
Typesetting: H&P Graphics Ltd
Colour separation:
by Scantrans PTE Ltd, Singapore
Printed:
by Proost International Book Production,
Turnhout, Belgium

The Author

Dr Richard Pagett is an environmental scientist specialising in environmental impact assessment. After gaining his PhD in Marine Ecology at the University of London, he was appointed Research Fellow at the University of Leeds, where he undertook research in marine chemistry until 1983. Since then, Dr Pagett has been involved in many environmental impact assessment projects on fish farming, oil and gas exploration and development, sewage disposal, tidal barrages and other civil engineering schemes.

Dr Pagett has contributed to a number of previous books, most notably on the subjects of water pollution control and the practice of scientific diving, and his papers have appeared in many journals. He lectures widely on environmental impact assessment, drawing on his experiences in the Caribbean and Middle East as well as in the United Kingdom.

Above: *The jellyfish* Orchistoma pileus. *Jellyfish are free floating and move with the wind and currents.*

CONTENTS

INTRODUCTION

The sea has fascinated man down the ages, from the inevitability of the rising and falling tide to the awesome power of waves crashing against the shore in a storm. This book is an introduction to the many aspects of the sea not apparent to the casual observer on the beach. It reveals a world of enormous variety and extraordinary forces, a world which holds much of importance for us on land.

With *environment* having been the watchword of the late eighties and continuing as such into the nineties, attention will remain focused on global concerns of an environmental nature – for example, the greenhouse effect, changing climate patterns, deforestation and acid rain. The seas and oceans cover more than two thirds of the world's surface, hence it is not surprising that they are closely tied in to these matters. Indeed, one of the principal consequences of global warming being forecast by many authorities is a significant rise in sea level. Such a development would be extremely damaging for mankind, and it is in our own interests that we attempt to understand better the forces concerned.

This book describes the fundamental mechanisms that operate in the seas and oceans. The movement of the ocean basins and the principal features of the ocean floor are described. Tides, waves and currents are examined, and how the surface of the oceans interacts with the atmosphere above and controls the weather is explained. Sea water itself and the reactions and cycles that take place within it are analysed. There is a description of the relatively recently discovered 'black smokers', 'white smokers' and warm-water vents. The variety of muds that coat the ocean floor – where they come from and their distribution – is described. There is a chapter on marine habitats and the life they support, from the shores at the ocean margin to the dark, cold water of the deep ocean. The fragile balance of nature that interlinks all the animals and plants of the sea is explained, and how that balance is threatened by man's exploitation of the ocean and its resources is examined. The final chapter focuses on some of the existing laws and management plans for safeguarding our ocean heritage.

It is hoped that this book will stimulate a general interest in younger readers and encourage them to find out more about the undersea world and its importance.

Right: *The sea at its most familiar – as enjoyed on a walk along the beach. The shore itself holds much of interest for the observant walker, yet in, under and even above the vast expanse of water stretching beyond the horizon, forces that defy the imagination are in constant operation.*

1 • Geology Under the Sea

STRUCTURE AND PROCESSES

The earth is made up of several layers of rock. The two main outer layers are the lithosphere and the aesthenosphere. The lithosphere lies immediately beneath the continents and the oceans. Under the continents it is about 150 miles (250km) thick, whereas under the oceans it is about 60 miles (100km) thick. The upper layer of the lithosphere is known as the crust. Underlying the lithosphere is the aesthenosphere, which is part of the mantle.

Movement of the earth's surface

It is only during the last thirty years or so that sufficient evidence has been gathered to support the view, now widely held, that the continents and ocean basins are not fixed features on the surface of the earth. It is now firmly believed that they have been moving through geological time and continue to do so today. The rate of movement is very slow – centimetres per year. As a result of this movement, scientists believe that the Atlantic and Indian Oceans are increasing in size while the Pacific Ocean is becoming smaller.

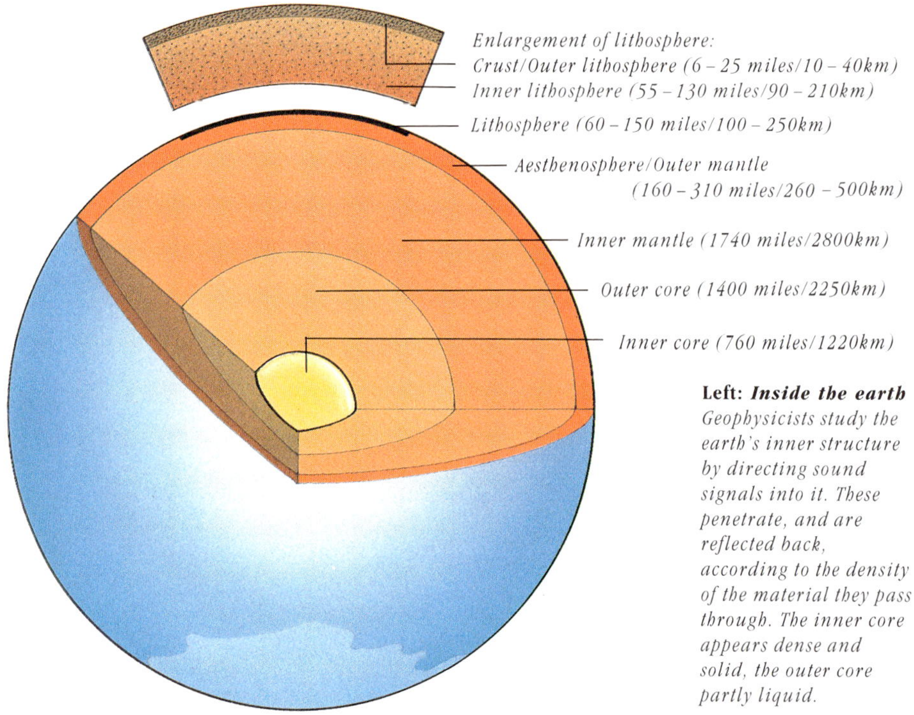

Left: *Inside the earth*
Geophysicists study the earth's inner structure by directing sound signals into it. These penetrate, and are reflected back, according to the density of the material they pass through. The inner core appears dense and solid, the outer core partly liquid.

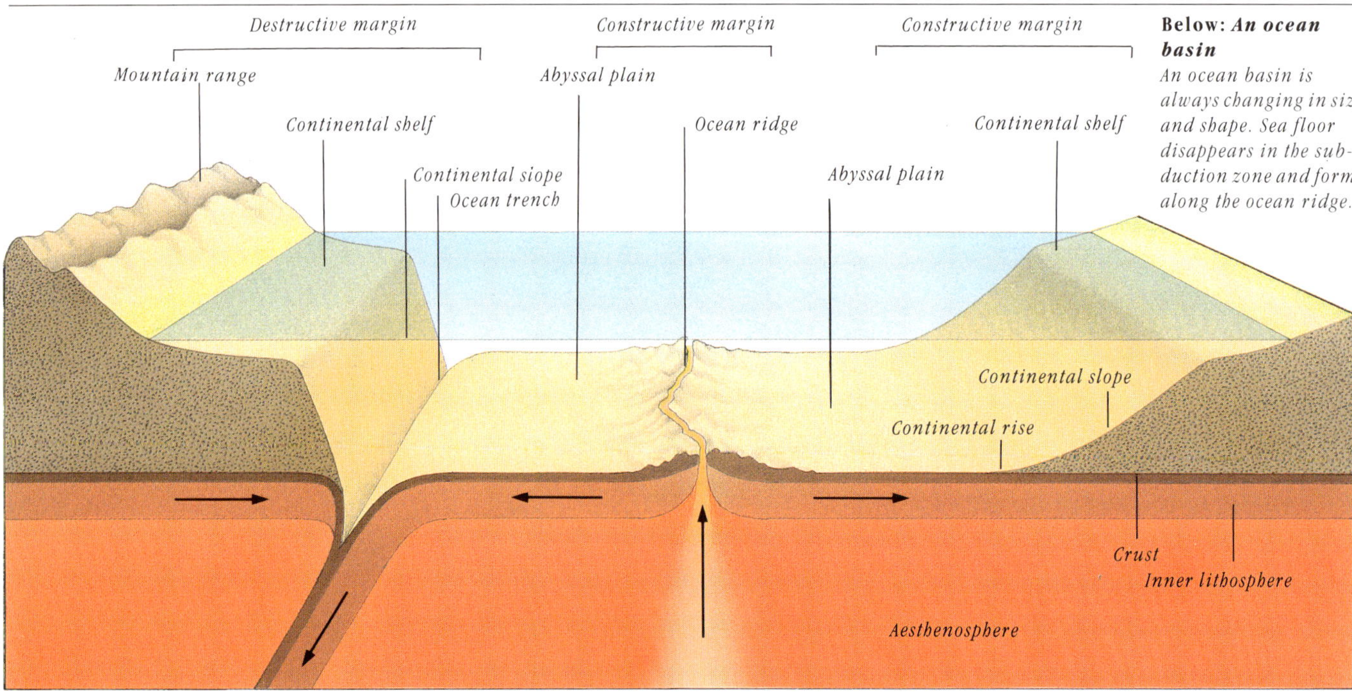

Below: *An ocean basin*
An ocean basin is always changing in size and shape. Sea floor disappears in the subduction zone and forms along the ocean ridge.

Plates

A number of expeditions and international projects, such as the Deep Sea Drilling Project of the 1960s, Project FAMOUS (French–American Mid-Ocean Undersea Study) of the 1970s, and the Ocean Drilling Project of the 1980s, have investigated various aspects of the earth's structure. These studies have helped geologists and geophysicists to understand something of the processes that have shaped, and continue to shape, the continents and ocean floor.

Scientists believe that the lithosphere consists of several plates or sections which are moving. On the surface of these plates are the continents and ocean basins. Some plates have both continent and ocean basin on them; others have only continent or only ocean basin.

Where two plates are pulling away from each other, material from the mantle is constantly rising to fill the space. This upwelling of material is effectively producing new sea floor; the process is known as sea-floor spreading.

Where two plates are colliding, one goes under the other (or is 'subducted') into the mantle. Ocean trenches form at the site of this process, which is known as subduction.

It is quite possible that in one area of the earth's crust a plate is being subducted while in another area the same plate is having material added to it by the process of sea-floor spreading. Clearly, if the rate of sea-floor spreading in the one area is greater than the rate of subduction in the other, there is a net increase in the size of the plate. If the converse is the case, there is a reduction in the size of the plate.

Features of the ocean bed

The sites along which the earth's crust is being subducted into the aesthenosphere are called destructive margins, and it is here that ocean trenches form. The sites along which sea-floor spreading is taking place are called constructive margins and appear as ridge-like formations rather like mountain ranges.

Between the ridges and the trenches lie the ocean plains (known also as abyssal plains). These are vast areas of sediment. Where the sediments pile up near to the continents, they form the continental shelves.

An approximate guide to the water depth in the different parts of the ocean is as follows: in the ocean trenches, possibly more than 35,000ft (10,000m); over the plains, around 20,000ft (6000m); over the continental shelves, about 650ft (200m).

GLORIA

Detailed maps of the ocean basins are needed for a number of purposes, including the understanding of physical processes, such as global water circulation, and exploration for physical resources, such as oil, sands and gravels, and mineral deposits. Maps are constructed using the technique of echo sounding.

Echo sounding employs the transmission and reception of a pulse of sound. Knowing the speed of sound through sea water, it is possible to calculate the distance that the received sound has travelled since bouncing off the sea bed. This distance is the depth of the water. The major disadvantage of this technique is that it only maps along a single line, corresponding to the cruise track of the survey vessel deploying the echo sounder. One would need, therefore, to map a lot of lines in order to build up a full picture of the sea bed. Survey vessels are very expensive to operate, however, so doing this would cost a great deal of money.

Side scan sonar relies on a principle similar to that of echo sounding. However, instead of sending out a sound pulse that, effectively, strikes the sea bed only at a single point, the sonar sends out a much wider signal.

GLORIA, which stands for Geological Long Range Asdic, is a sophisticated side scan sonar approximately 26ft (8m) long. It is towed about 1000ft (300m) behind the survey vessel at a speed of about ten knots and at a depth of 160ft (50m) below the surface.

In water about 16,000ft (5000m) deep, GLORIA is able to provide a reflected signal from a strip of sea bed about 40 miles (60km) wide. By overlapping several strips, features such as submarine canyons, mud slides, sea mounts, volcanoes (see right-hand photograph) and nodule fields and other metal deposits can be observed.

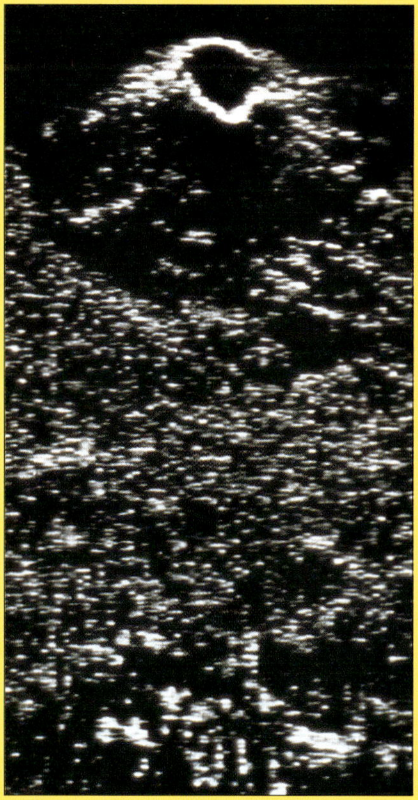

CONTINENTAL MARGINS

There are two types of continental margin: the Atlantic and the Pacific. Those of the Atlantic type are characterised by having little earthquake activity associated with them. They are known as aseismic, passive or constructive margins. With this type of margin the continent and the ocean basin are on the same plate.

Continental margins of the Pacific type are characteristically associated with substantial earthquake activity. This is because they are formed where an oceanic plate is being subducted under a continental plate. They are known as seismic, active or destructive margins. With this type, the continental mass and the ocean basin are on different plates. A continental trench occurs at the foot of the continental slope, and the edge of the adjacent continental mass generally features a mountain range thrown up by volcanic activity along the site of subduction.

Continental margins round the Indian Ocean are mainly of the Atlantic type, although there is an exception to this in the north-east as indicated by the presence of the Java Trench.

Sediment transport

With the Atlantic type of margin, the continental shelf may be as wide as 900 miles (1500km). This is owing to the expanse of accumulated sediment washed off the adjacent continental mass. This sediment flows gently down the continental slope before settling.

In many areas the continental slope is cut by submarine canyons. These are scoured out by sediment-laden flows called turbidity currents, often extensions of major rivers. A turbidity current is set in motion when a heavy suspension, or thick soup, of sediment accumulates on the slope. Once there is insufficient friction to hold it in place, it breaks loose. Because it is denser than sea water, a turbidity current flows down the continental slope under its own weight until its momentum is overcome by the decreasing gradient. The sediments then pile up to form the continental rise.

There are cases in which less sediment has accumulated at the foot of the continental slope than might have been expected. This is generally believed to be because there is insufficient rainfall in the area to produce the run-off from the nearby continental mass necessary to carry substantially greater quantities of sediment to the sea in the first place.

With the Pacific type of margin, the sediments washed off the adjacent continent and which flow gently down the continental slope are trapped by the ocean trench. This results in the continental rise being much sharper than along the Atlantic type of margin.

Island arcs

Ocean trenches, which may be as deep as 7 miles (11km), are associated not only with continental margins of the Pacific type (i.e. where an oceanic plate is being subducted under a continental plate). They form also where one oceanic plate is moving under another, and in such cases island arcs also form. These are offshore mountain chains thrown up along the site of subduction, believed to be equivalent to the mountain ranges along continental margins of the Pacific type. In both instances the plate that is being subducted melts, and the molten material contributes to the continental mountains and, it is thought, to the island arcs as well. More and more is being discovered all the time about the origins of island arcs.

Below: ***Formation of an island arc***

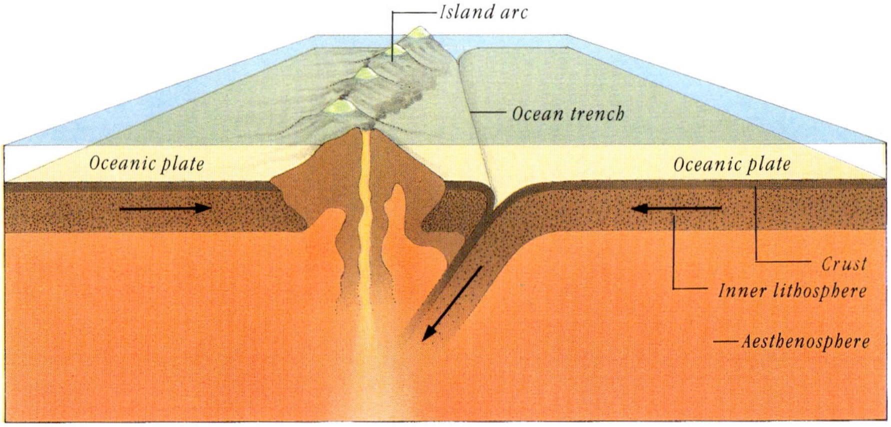

Below: ***Comparison of continental slopes***

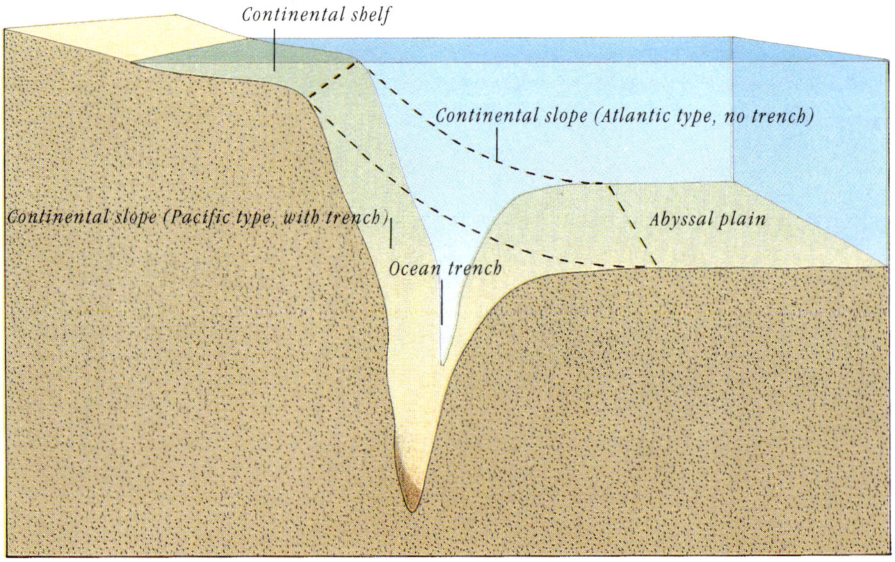

OCEAN RIDGES

Ocean ridges are major features of the ocean floor. They are formed of new sea-floor material, which wells up where two plates are pulling away from each other. The new material is added to each plate equally and generally lies perpendicular to (i.e. across) the axis of the ridge. A ridge may extend in places across a third of the breadth of an ocean's floor, reaching as high as 2½ miles (4km).

Rates of spread

The rate of addition is not constant. In the Atlantic Ocean it is of the order of ⅖in (1cm) a year, while in the Pacific Ocean it is much quicker, about 2½–3in (6–8cm) a year. Consequently, the Mid-Atlantic Ridge is called a slow-spreading ridge, and the East Pacific Rise is called a fast-spreading ridge. The width of a slow-spreading ridge might be around 1250 miles (2000km), while that of a fast-spreading ridge might be as much as 2500 miles (4000km).

The different rates of spreading give different outward appearances to the ridges. The slow-spreading ridges of the Atlantic Ocean have a flat bottom and a generally rougher surface relief than do the fast-spreading ridges of the Pacific Ocean.

Temperature and depth

The new sea-floor material is very hot at the centre of a ridge and gradually cools down as it spreads outwards. While hot it is buoyant, being less dense than when cool (rather like hot water in a domestic hot-water tank, which rises and sits above the cold). As it cools it contracts and loses its buoyancy. Consequently, the water depth increases with distance from the centre of the ridge.

Faults

Another distinctive feature of the ridges is the presence of transform faults, which occur where oceanic plates are slipping past each other. At these sites there is generally no material being added to the edge of either plate (although there may be exceptions to this). The faults lie parallel to the direction of movement of the plates and are seismically active. They run from axis to axis, and may extend into the plates as fracture zones. There is little or no seismic activity associated with these fracture zones.

Above: *As hot lava rises out of the magma chamber and meets the cold sea water, it forms a skin and then solidifies. As it solidifies, it forms rounded mounds, known as pillow lava. The mounds are similar in shape to toothpaste as it is squeezed out of a tube.*

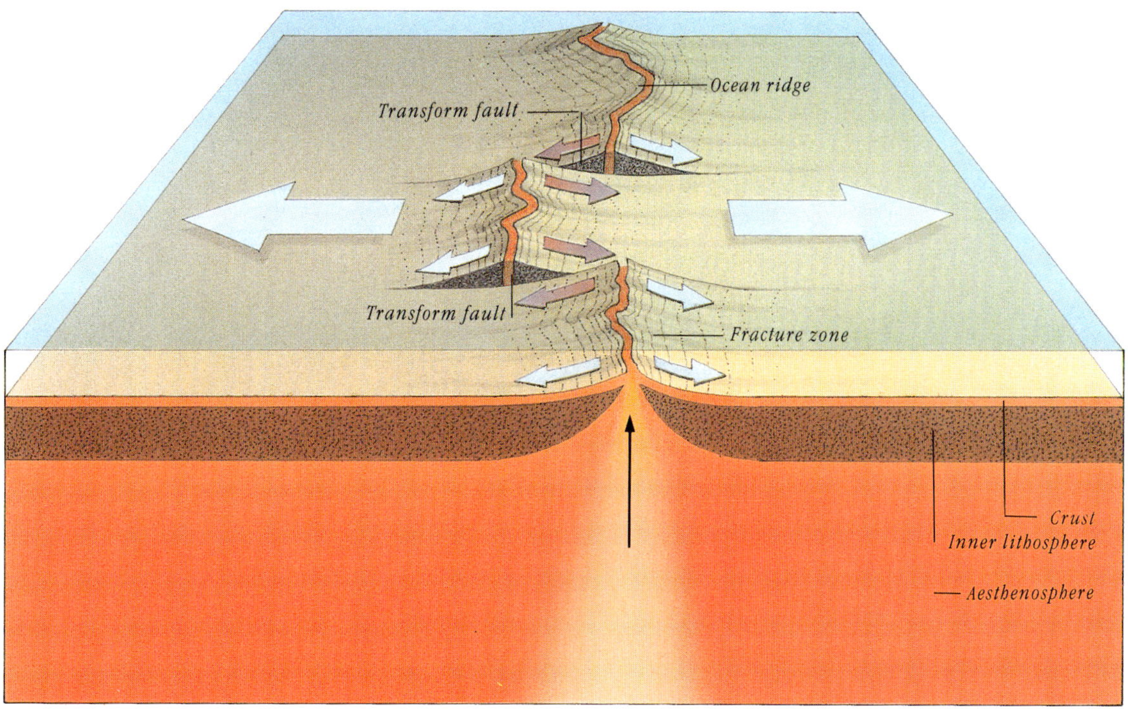

Right: *Transform faults*
The arrows indicate the direction of movement of the two plates. Note how the edges of the two plates can slip past each other (red arrows), yet new sea floor is added only to the trailing edge of each plate.

PLAINS AND TRENCHES

The deep-ocean floor lies between the continental margins and the ocean ridges and occupies more than 40 per cent of the oceanic area. Much of it is featureless. The two major provinces are the abyssal plains and the oceanic trenches.

Abyssal plains

The abyssal plains are extremely flat, almost flatter than anywhere else on Earth. Gradients seldom rise or fall more than 3ft (1m) over a distance of a mile (1.5km). There are, however, some exceptions to this general flatness. There are hills and mountains, both of which are considered to be volcanic in origin. Hills are defined as less than 3000ft (1000m) in height, mountains as more than this. Interestingly, these hills and mountains do not rise up off the plain gradually, but very abruptly. This is thought to be because their true bases are buried deep under the sediment of the plain.

There is an increase in gradient on passing from the plains to the rise of the continental margins. In the other direction, the plains extend to where the ridges are forming. The surface relief of the ridges can be obscured completely by burial under the masses of sediment that have accumulated.

The abyssal plains of the Atlantic Ocean are substantially more extensive than those of the Pacific Ocean because much of the sediment transported into the latter is trapped by the oceanic trenches and the island arcs.

Oceanic trenches

The deepest parts of the ocean are the trenches. The Marianas Trench in the western Pacific reaches a depth of about 35,000ft (11,000m). In cross-section the trenches are partly V-shaped and partly flat at the base. Just why this is so is not clear, especially when it is recalled that oceanic trenches are forming at the sites where one plate is being subducted beneath another. Further geophysical investigation will be needed before scientists can put an explanation to this.

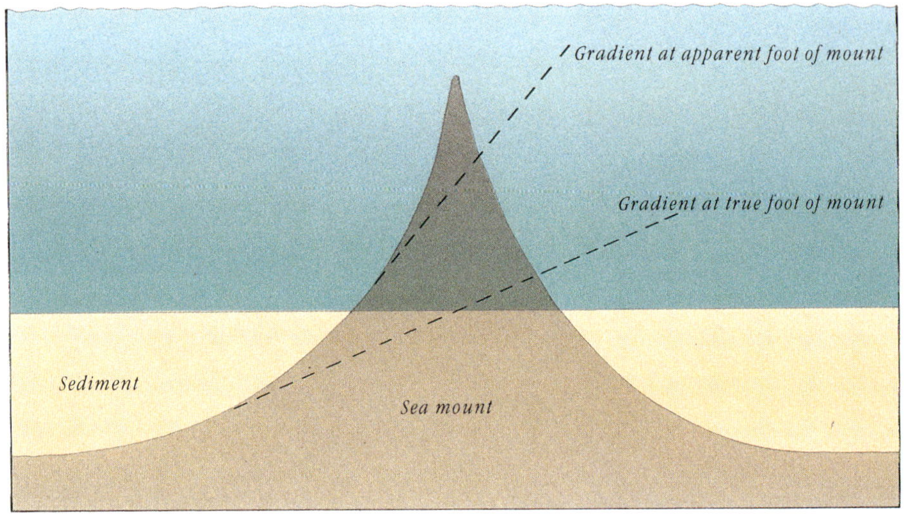

Above: ***Gradient of a sea mount***

Above: *Note how the base of the sea mount is covered by sediment which obscures its true shape.*

Right: *The top of this volcano in the Galapagos may one day be flat and beneath the surface of the sea. See* ***Guyot formation*** *opposite.*

SEA MOUNTS AND VOLCANOES

Most sea mounts are volcanoes rising up from the ocean floor, although many do not reach as far as the surface. They are more apparent in the Pacific Ocean than in the Atlantic, there being less sediment on the floor of the Pacific (because so much is trapped by the trenches) to obscure or bury them. Sea mounts may occur together in chains or as isolated peaks. Their slopes can be very steep - steeper than any other feature in the ocean - and the mounts themselves can be extremely large. For instance, Mauna Loa in the islands of Hawaii measures more than 60 miles (100km) across its base and is as tall as Mount Everest.

Many sea mounts appear to have formed at or near a region of sea-floor spreading and originally to have reached the surface. They then subsided as the new sea floor cooled and contracted on moving away from the centre of the ridge.

Guyots

Some sea mounts have flat tops. This is generally thought to be a consequence of wave and wind action having eroded the rock when the tops were at or above sea level. Another theory, however, is that these mounts are old volcanoes the craters of which have filled up with lava. Flat-topped sea mounts are known as guyots. Conforming to the theory that as the hot sea-floor material moves away from the spreading centre it cools and therefore contracts, the older guyots are found further from the centre and in deeper water than the younger guyots.

In keeping, too, with the theory that guyots at one time reached the surface of the ocean, many present-day coral reef atolls appear to be built on the tops of these sea mounts. Drilling down through coral reefs has shown that some are founded on very old platforms. It would seem that the tops of the guyots were colonised by corals and other reef organisms when at the surface, and the rate of reef growth has since kept pace with the descent of the guyots. There is one undersea mountain range that has been found to have coral reefs along its top dating from as far back as the Cretaceous period (which lasted from 135 to 65 million years ago).

It has been suggested that the supposedly lost city of Atlantis was actually built on a guyot that had reached the surface. Of course, as the guyot eventually sank below the waves, the fabled city disappeared. There is no scientific evidence of such a civilisation on any of the guyots studied so far; but there are many guyots that have yet to be explored...

Hot spots

It is intriguing that while many submarine volcanoes are scattered, others appear in chain formation. Some volcanoes are active, too, while others are dormant. One explanation is that as an area of a plate moves over a local heat source, or hot spot, a dormant volcano becomes active before dying down once more as that particular area of the plate moves away from the hot spot. In other places, the heat source is linear and is thought to be responsible for chains, such as the Walvis Rise in the south Atlantic.

Above: *Coral atolls of the Maldive Islands, in the Indian Ocean. Atolls are thought to form round the tops of volcanoes. If a volcano is on a plate that is moving away from a centre of spreading and is therefore cooling and contracting, it sinks. As the volcano sinks, the coral maintains its position at the surface by growing upwards. Some Maldive atolls are 400ft (120m) thick.*

Below: ***Guyot formation***
The diagram shows how the top of a sea mount can be flattened by wave erosion. As the plate it is on moves away from the hot centre of spreading, the mount cools, contracts and sinks beneath the surface.

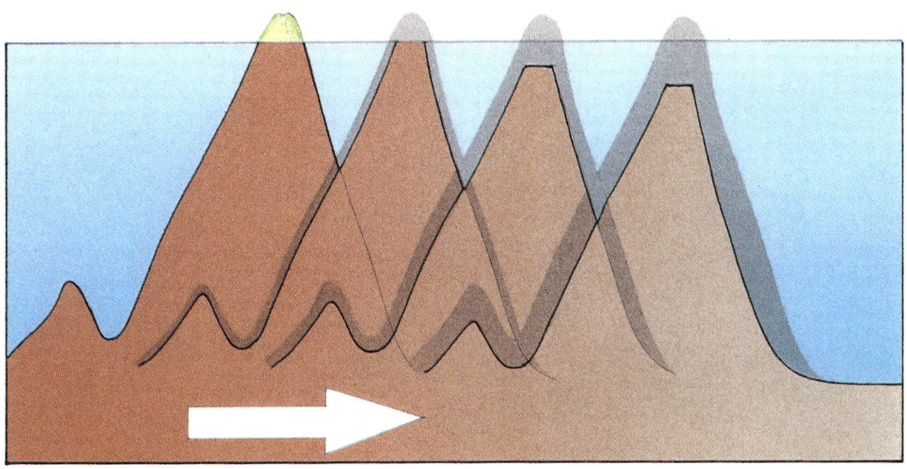

2·Physics of the Sea

WATER MOVEMENTS

The movement of water in the form of tides, currents and waves underlies many of the processes that take place in the oceans, from the surface down to the bottom of the ocean trenches.

Tides

Tides operate as a result of the attraction of the moon and the sun. Their attraction pulls the water on the earth's surface towards them. Because the moon is much closer than the sun to the earth, its pull is much stronger. When the moon and the sun are directly in line with each other and the earth, their pull is greatest and the highest and lowest tides occur (spring tides). Conversely, when they attract at right angles to each other, their pull is weakest and the tides display the smallest rise and fall (neap tides). Spring tides and neap tides each occur twice a month (really every twenty-eight-day lunar cycle). There is a high and low tide twice each day with about six hours between high and low water.

If a coastline has a very long, narrow inlet set into it, the rising tide in the inlet may be restricted. Gradually, as the tide rises, the water piles up at the mouth of the inlet until it suddenly rushes through as a wave. This wave is called a tidal bore. Good examples of this phenomenon can be seen in the Bay of Fundy, Newfoundland, and in the estuary of the River Severn in England.

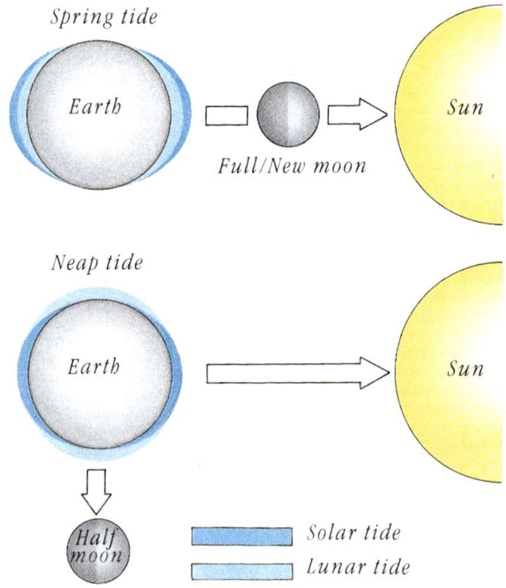

Above: *Tide generation*
The two generators of tides are the moon and sun. At a given point on a shore, the time of high water is progressively later each day. This is because of the moon's change in position relative to the earth during the course of each month.

Currents

Ocean currents are generated as a result of the combined effects of wind, atmospheric pressure and variations in density in different parts of the sea. These variations in density reflect differences in heat exchange between the atmosphere and the surface of the sea. This exchange, in turn, affects the evaporation and dilution of the surface water.

Once currents are generated, the paths they follow are determined by the rotation of the earth and by the shape of the ocean basins and continents.

The Trade Winds drive the North and South Equatorial Currents, which flow from east to west across the Atlantic Ocean. As the currents approach land they are turned to the north and south respectively. In the north Atlantic,

Right: *Major ocean currents*
Warm currents are shown as red, cold currents as blue. The current shown as stippled occupies a northerly position in the Northern winter and a southerly one in summer

1 *Gulf Stream*
2 *Labrador*
3 *East Greenland*
4 *North Atlantic Drift*
5 *Canary*
6 *North Equatorial*
7 *Brazil*
8 *Benguela*
9 *Antarctic Circumpolar*
10 *Peru*
11 *South Equatorial*
12 *West Australian*
13 *Agulhas*
14 *Kuroshio*
15 *California*
16 *Oyashio*
17 *North Pacific*
18 *Antarctic Subpolar*

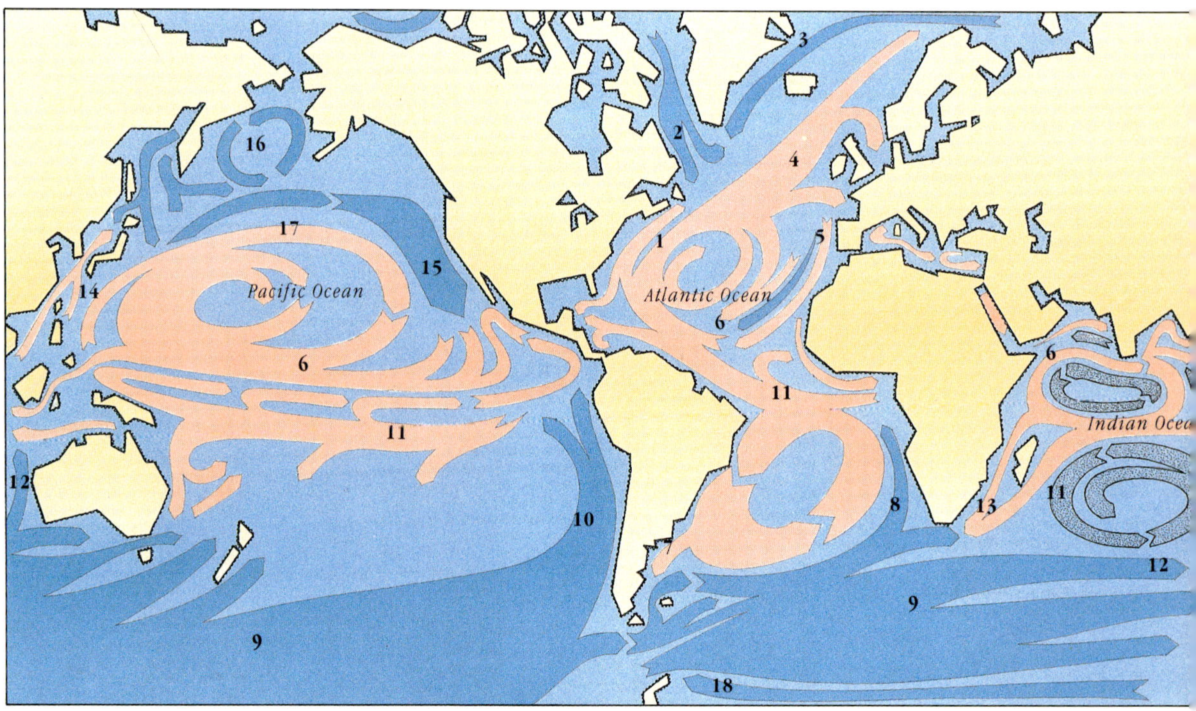

the North Equatorial Current flows into the Gulf of Mexico, from where it emerges and flows west as the Gulf Stream. This current is eventually deflected again, by the land mass of Europe, and travels south to rejoin the Equatorial Currents. Inside this circular movement is an area of calm water with little current, the Sargasso Sea.

Not all the Gulf Stream is turned ultimately to the south. Some eventually enters the Arctic Ocean to the north, the inflowing water balanced by a similar volume of outflowing water. The cooler outflow passes under the warmer inflow.

In the south Atlantic, the South Equatorial Current contributes to a circulation opposite to that in the north. In the Pacific and Indian Oceans, the surface currents are broadly similar in pattern, although in the latter the picture is complicated by the monsoon period.

Currents do not occur only at the surface. Water returning to the equator is generally cooler than water leaving the warm regions and therefore flows at depth.

An ocean current should not be visualised as a steady progression, rather as a swirling transport of water of a particular character (e.g. with a certain range of temperature and of salinity) to an area where it merges with water of a different character.

Waves

Most waves arise because of the movement of wind over the surface of the sea. Some of the more dramatic waves occur as a result of geological movement, such as those caused by submarine volcanoes and earthquakes.

As the wind passes over the sea, it generates small undulations in the surface called ripples, which gradually increase in size to become wind waves. The distance from the crest of one wind wave to that of another may be more than 1000ft (300m). Waves gradually move forwards from where they are formed at speeds of up to 60 mph (100km/hr). Waves that have moved well away from where they were formed, perhaps during a storm, cause what is generally known as 'swell'.

As waves approach the coast, they tend to change direction and approach at an angle. Entering shallow water, a wave's base makes contact with the sea bed and follows any undulations in it. As the wave passes into very shallow water, its base is slowed down by friction with the bed. The crest of the wave, now travelling much faster than the base, eventually falls forwards and surges up the shore. The surge water returns to the sea either by seeping into the beach material and draining back through it or by washing back down the shore.

The tidal waves of the disaster movies have very little to do with tides. They are generally caused by some great geological movement – volcanic activity or earthquake. They are known technically as 'tsunamis'. When the sea bed rises and falls suddenly, as during a submarine earthquake, the water above it moves in response and a series of waves is set up. Probably the best-known example is the tsunami that accompanied the volcanic eruption of Krakatoa, between Java and Sumatra, in 1883. The effect of this travelled right round the globe.

Tsunami is a Japanese word, reflecting the fact that these waves are more usual in the Pacific Ocean, arising from activity connected with sites such as Kamchatka, the Aleutian Trench and the area off Chile. Europe also experiences tsunamis. Faulting off the Mid-Atlantic Ridge near the Azores generated a tsunami that swept up the Tagus estuary in Portugal with great loss of life in 1755.

Right: *These waves were formed far out in the Atlantic Ocean during a storm and probably travelled hundreds of miles before being obstructed by the coast of Cornwall, in south-east England. Much of their energy and thus destructive power will have been dissipated by their passage over the ocean surface.*

Measurement of currents

Currents were originally determined using drift bottles. The path of a current can be traced if these, each containing a note to whoever finds it, are released in large numbers to travel with the current. The locations at which returned bottles are found can be plotted on a chart. A variation on this is the use of carefully ballasted devices which hang below the surface or near the sea bed. Strongly coloured dye can also be used, although wind affects this more easily. Current meters (see photograph), placed in a fixed position, can record the speed and direction of a current on magnetic tape or on solid-state memory using electromagnetic sensors.

CIRCULATION AND ATMOSPHERE

Oceanic circulation is extremely complex. There are two masses of cold, dense water, one in the northern hemisphere (the Norwegian and Greenland Seas), the other in the southern hemisphere (the Weddell Sea). Because these waters have cooled and increased in density, they sink, becoming the North Atlantic Deep Water and the Antarctic Bottom Water respectively. These two masses then flow along the western margin of the Atlantic Ocean, the one in a southerly direction, the other in a northerly direction. The Antarctic Bottom Water also flows round the Antarctic, supplying cold, deep-ocean water to the Indo-Pacific Ocean. Here it flows in a northerly direction, also along the western margin of the ocean.

Owing to easterly drifting, these currents gradually upwell over a wide area, replenishing the upper, warmer waters with nutrients. In certain coastal areas, this upwelling is responsible for concentrated biological production. Once at the surface, the upwelled waters are directed by the winds (see pages 14–15 and 20) and eventually return to the polar regions, where they cool, increase in density and sink once again.

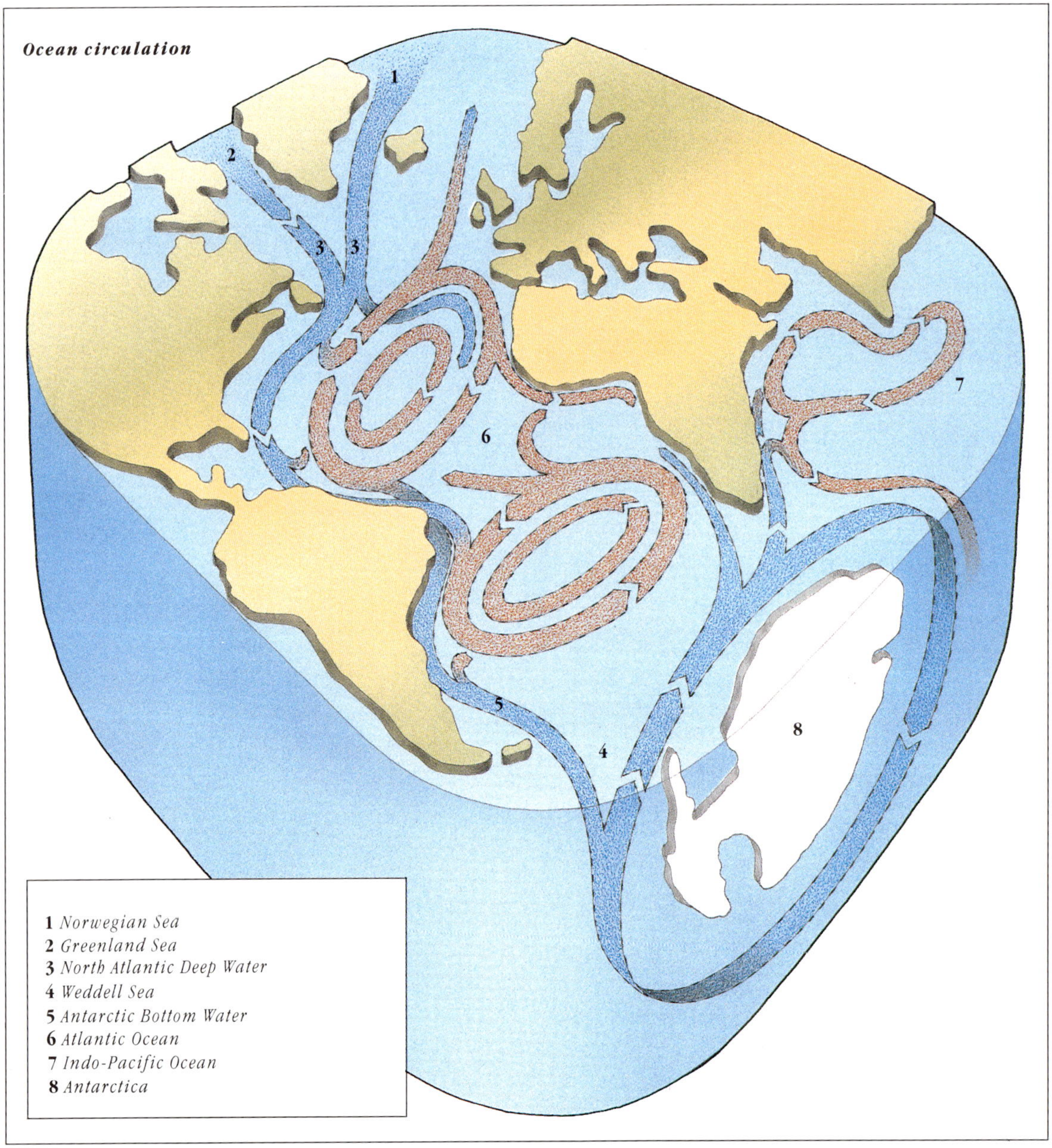

Right: *This rain squall in the South Pacific Ocean is on the move and will be over a quite different part of the sea in just a few hours. Its effect on the water it passes over will last for days. The turbulence it creates at the surface may influence the rate at which gases such as carbon dioxide and oxygen are exchanged between the atmosphere and the ocean water.*

Right: *This is an aerial view of Hurricane Elena. The swirling pattern of cloud is caused by the wind, which is producing similar patterns in the ocean water below. It is not just the surface of the ocean which is affected – the storm may be felt many tens of metres down. In shallow areas, whole coral reef systems can be devastated by the passage of such storms.*

Coupling of the ocean and atmosphere

The weather changes week by week, day by day, even hour by hour. The turbulent features of the atmosphere can be observed in the ocean, but because of the viscosity of water, changes in the ocean are much slower. For instance, water of the North Atlantic takes up to ten years to circulate around the ocean basin, yet an equivalent air circulation, such as that caused by a storm, takes a few weeks at the most. The exchange of warm surface water with cool deep-ocean water may take tens or hundreds of years.

Such gradual change imposes a general stability on ocean processes. The ocean surface, however, is 'coupled' with the atmosphere – that is, is in intimate contact with it. This can bring about certain far-reaching short-term changes, both in the ocean and on land. For example, the phenomenon known as El Niño (see page 21) can change the circulation of the surface waters of the tropical Pacific Ocean, and is thought to have caused the 1988 American Midwest drought.

The greenhouse effect

A major topic of public concern since the late eighties has been that of global warming, popularly known as the greenhouse effect. Carbon dioxide and other gases, produced in unnaturally large quantities by certain of Man's activities, are accumulating in the atmosphere. Here they are trapping heat from the sun which would, under natural conditions, be reflected off the earth's surface and back through the atmosphere into space (much as a greenhouse traps the sun's heat). Some estimates predict an average global temperature rise of as much as 9°F (5°C) during the twenty-first century. In determining future temperatures around the globe, however, it is difficult to evaluate the effect of the coupling of the ocean and atmosphere. The ocean has a greater heat-carrying capacity than the atmosphere (which is why the sea always feels warmer in the evening than during the day) and takes longer to heat up and cool down than the air. This slow response of the ocean to changes in atmospheric temperature may have important implications for the outlook on global warming. Furthermore, the ocean holds as much as fifty times more carbon dioxide than the atmosphere, so is important in regulating the amount of carbon dioxide in the atmosphere.

The question, then, is will the ocean absorb the accumulating heat and carbon dioxide or will these remain in the atmosphere? Some basic mechanisms have still to be understood before this can be answered with any certainty. One such mechanism concerns the role of phytoplankton, the microscopic green plants that grow near the ocean surface. As atmospheric carbon dioxide increases, there is an increase in carbon dioxide in the surface waters of the ocean. This stimulates higher plankton productivity, which increases production of the gas dimethyl sulphide. This gas escapes to the atmosphere, where it changes chemically and associates with dust particles. This association stimulates cloud production. Clouds block out some of the sun's heat and thus check, to a degree, the warming of the atmosphere.

Coupling of the ocean and atmosphere involves many regulatory processes of this kind. Scientists need to understand these, and their interaction, better.

SEA LEVEL AND CLIMATE

Sea level has never been constant for long; it has always been changing. Changes in sea level result from a number of global processes. The freezing and melting of glaciers trap and release water respectively. Water masses themselves contract or expand with changes in internal temperature. As new sea-floor material spreads out from the site of its upwelling, it cools. As it cools, it contracts, thereby enlarging the oceanic basin and causing a fall in sea level. Other processes are more local, such as those affecting geological stability of an area, e.g. land uplift or subsidence.

Scientists believe climates have been fairly stable for the last 5000 years, and that the sea level around the globe has changed by no more than 3ft (1m) up or down. Where greater changes have apparently occurred locally, they are considered to be the result of land uplifting or subsiding, not the sea falling or rising. Data compiled over many years suggest the global sea level has risen 4–5in (10–13cm) in the last 100 years – an average rate of 0.016–0.02in (0.04–0.06cm) per year. However, there is wide variation between this and other estimates.

Why is there variation, and who is right? In order to determine sea level changes accurately, it is necessary to know more about those processes (outlined above) that bring them about. This knowledge then needs to be expressed mathematically and built into models which simulate mathematically what happens in nature. At present, such models rely too much on assumptions about the processes concerned, not hard and fast knowledge. Assumptions vary, hence estimates vary also.

Global warming

Global warming arises from the production of certain gases which encircle the earth and trap the sun's heat. These gases include carbon dioxide and nitrous oxide from the burning of wood and fossil fuels; chlorofluorocarbons, used in refrigerators, aerosol cans and some industrial processes; and methane, produced in the digestive tract of cows and in rice paddies. Green plants absorb carbon dioxide, but as forests in certain parts of the world (e.g. in the Amazon area of South America) are cut down for fuel and to clear land for farming, fewer plants remain to do this.

Global warming is sure to bring about an expansion of the oceans as glaciers and the ice caps melt. Perhaps there is little risk to those living in low-lying areas for the next fifteen years or so, but after that? No one knows for sure. Protecting coastal cities, shorelines and wetlands would cost a great deal of money. Some recent estimates suggest that an increase in temperature of between 3 and 11°F (1.5 and 6°C) can be anticipated within the next hundred years, which could mean a rise in sea level of 3–6ft (1–2m). An area like the Maldives, a group of over 1100 island atolls in the Indian Ocean none of which is more than 6ft (2m) above sea level, is in obvious danger of being completely submerged.

Far right: *Glaciers such as this, in Greenland, lock up a considerable amount of water which will be released as air and sea temperatures increase.*

Right: *Rising sea levels will threaten coral islands like this in the Maldives. Even in 1987, flooding inundated many small islands of the Maldives.*

Rising sea level

Low-lying delta regions will feel most a rise in sea level. Natural patterns of sediment accumulation and subsidence in these regions are often disrupted by man: e.g. extraction of groundwater, as in Thailand, lowers the water table, thereby increasing subsidence.

Bangladesh is a small Asian country on the world's largest deltaic plain – the Bengal Delta. This delta accounts for 80% of the country's surface area, hence Bangladesh already suffers annual flooding. Irrigation and groundwater removal have contributed to a lack of sediment accumulation and increased subsidence, worsening matters. Recent calculations suggest the sea may rise 27in (70cm) by the middle of next century, covering 18% of the habitable land of Bangladesh and displacing 17 million people. By century's end, the number could be 38 million.

Persons displaced in this way by changes in the environment are known as environmental refugees.

UPWELLING AND FISHERIES

When the wind blows from the land over the sea, it can cause the surface water along the coast to move in the same direction, i.e. out to sea. This water is replaced by water drawn up from the deeper regions of the ocean, a process known as upwelling. Coastal upwelling occurs in several parts of the world, notably the Canaries, western Africa, Peru, California, western Australia and near the Antarctic.

The upward-moving water can travel at about 3ft (1m) a day, and brings with it high concentrations of nutrients, principally nitrate and phosphate. These make up the food of the microscopic phytoplankton near the surface, themselves the first link in what is termed the food chain. (See below.)

In temperate regions, during the cooler times of the year, the surface water near the coast may cool. This causes the water to increase in density and therefore to sink down the continental shelf, a movement known as cascading. As the water cascades, it is replaced, sometimes by water less rich in nutrients. This leaves the phytoplankton at the surface short of food.

The food chain

Upwelling causes intense biological productivity. The nutrients brought up allow the phytoplankton to grow and reproduce. The phytoplankton are eaten by microscopic animals called zooplankton; these are eaten in turn by other, larger zooplankton and small fish. The larger zooplankton and small fish are eaten by larger fish, and these are eaten by still larger fish, and so on – a progression known as the food chain.

Peruvian anchovies

All upwelling areas in the oceans support extensive fisheries. One of the principal areas of upwelling is along the coast of Peru, which produces nearly a quarter of all fish caught worldwide. The Peruvian fishery is based on a species no more than a few centimetres in length – the anchovy. Although small, the anchovy can occur in its millions, forming huge schools in the current that flows northwards along the Peruvian coast.

As the water moves northwards, it veers away from the land. It is replaced by the upwelling of offshore water flowing at depth in a southerly direction. The upwelling water brings with it vast quantities of nutrients. Through the progression of the food chain, the nutrients support the populations of phytoplankton, zooplankton and, of course, anchovies.

Above: *Anchovies form huge schools in cold coastal waters, where they fall prey to larger fish, squid, guano birds and fishermen. The last of these is by far the greatest threat. Their purse seine nets can catch as much as 100 tonnes in a single cast. In a good year, the total fish stock may be of the order of 15–20 million tonnes.*

Right: *The anchovy trawlers of Peru are part of an industry that began in the late 1950s. Much of their catch is processed into fish meal, which is exported for enriching livestock feed, e.g. for poultry. Fish oil is also produced, for use in margarine, paint and cosmetics.*

El Niño

During its history, this highly valuable fishery has been struck by dramatic declines of population. A poorly understood series of meteorological and ocean conditions arises under which a warm, southerly flow of water travels along the coast. Being warm, this water flows above the cooler north-flowing current, which is thus slowed down and even stopped. The deeper, nutrient-rich water, therefore, cannot upwell, and the supply of nutrients so important to the phytoplankton, and ultimately to the anchovy, is cut off. As a result, the anchovy population crashes.

Because the warmer, southerly flowing current often appears around Christmas-time, the local fishermen have called it 'El Niño', Spanish for 'The Child'. El Niño occurs sporadically, perhaps two or three years in a row and then not for a further ten years or more. In an El Niño year, the winds come from the west rather than the more usual south-east.

One of the more severe El Niño years was 1972, when the surface temperature of the coastal water rose from its typical 72°F (22°C) to 86°F (30°C). So dramatic was this temperature rise that it took nearly twelve months for the water temperature to return to normal. Scientists remain puzzled by the 1972 anchovy population crash, however, since the decline seemed to begin before the water temperature was obviously rising.

More recently, El Niño has been linked to a wider phenomenon called the Southern Oscillation. This involves a change in the prevailing westerly Trade Winds across the Pacific Ocean. The winds build up in strength, then diminish. Water that has been shifted westwards by the winds then 'sloshes' back towards the west coast of South America, this movement becoming in effect part of the El Niño event. Such is the severity of this combined event that it can create climatic changes in coastal areas all around the Pacific, not just around Peru.

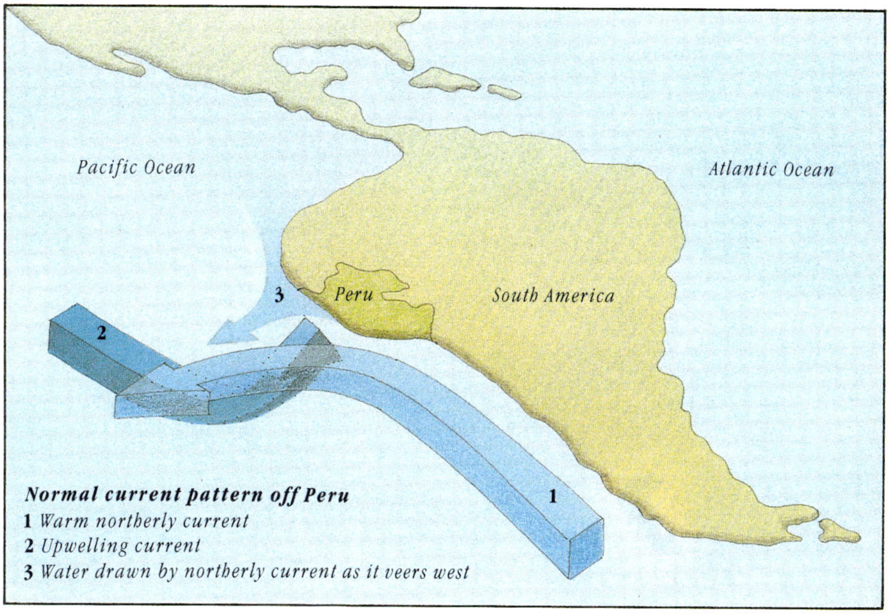

Above: *Offshore winds drive the northerly current away from land. Nutrient-rich water replaces it.*

Below: *The southerly current holds back the northerly flow and thus prevents upwelling.*

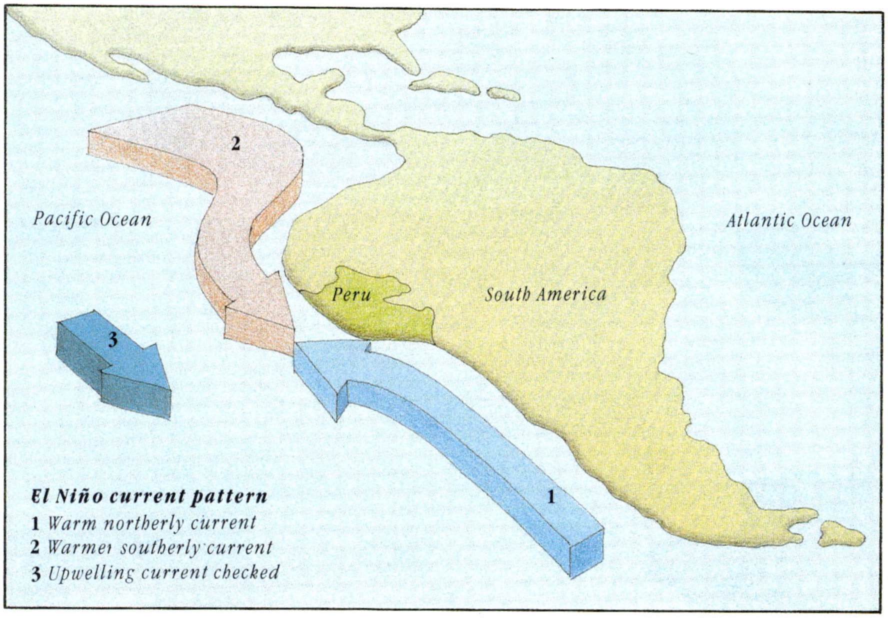

3·CHEMISTRY OF THE SEA

COMPOSITION OF SEA WATER

Probably the earliest discovery a child makes on his or her first visit to the seaside is that sea water is salty. The saltiness is caused by the presence of many different chemicals, not just salt itself. Some of these chemicals occur in quite high concentrations, others are found only in the minutest quantities. There are eleven major chemical constituents of sea water, but nearly every known element that occurs naturally on the planet has been found in the ocean.

There are on average about 6oz of 'salt' in every gallon of sea water (about 35g per litre). The saltiness (or salinity, to use the scientific term) is lower in areas where sea water is diluted by substantial rain or snow, or by a river entering the sea. In other areas, intense heat from the sun causes evaporation of water, leaving the remaining water more concentrated in salt. Water of a lower salinity is less dense than water of a higher salinity; the former therefore floats on the latter, and freshwater floats on sea water.

The elements found on land are added to sea water through the weathering of land rocks and the transport of sediment by rivers to the sea. In addition to these chemicals, however, the atmospheric gases are also found in the oceans. Oxygen is present in enormous quantities, although the surface waters contain rather more than the deeper regions. It is produced near the surface by the activity of phytoplankton. It is also found there as a result of exchange processes between the ocean surface and the atmosphere, which is rich in oxygen. This exchange is enhanced during storms because of the stirring and mixing action (turbulence) they cause. Carbon dioxide is the most abundant gas in sea water, however. With nitrate, it is vital for the plant growth that takes place at the ocean surface.

Above: *These bathers are floating in the highly saline water of the Dead Sea, in Israel. They can do so with ease because the high salt content increases the density of the water far in excess of the normal density of sea water.*

Right: *In the hot, dry desert air, the process of evaporation has left behind these salt formations along the edge of the Dead Sea.*

Nitrate, phosphate and silicate occur in quite high concentrations and are all important for the growth of plants. Other chemicals are found only in extremely low concentrations yet are crucial for the maintenance and well-being of marine plants and animals. For instance, iron, zinc and copper are essential to plants, copper and vanadium to animals. The precise roles of these chemicals is not always clear, yet often they are needed only in trace quantities. Some, such as vanadium, are concentrated by marine organisms; others, such as manganese, accumulate within sediments.

In addition to all these chemicals, there is also present in sea water an enormous quantity of particles. Either these are derived from the processes of erosion on land, or they are tiny fragments of organic matter that result from the breakdown after death of plankton and larger animals and plants.

GEOCHEMICAL PROCESSES

There are a number of processes that take place throughout the oceans and help to make the ocean as a whole the stable environment that it is. The ocean is neither gaining nor losing salt overall. Removal is balanced by addition. Any changes that do take place are gradual and measurable over a period of years.

The processes are interlinked. The salt in the sea is supplied mostly by the weathering of rocks on land. Fragments and particles so produced are carried to the sea by rivers or as dust in the air. Rainwater is a dilute version of sea water, its droplets carrying chemicals. Salt is also supplied by hydrothermal events and by volcanic activity both under the water and on land. The particles produced by these activities dissolve in the water and take part in many chemical and biological reactions. These reactions occur on and just below the sea bed as well as in the water itself.

There are also reactions at the ocean surface between it and the atmosphere. The air–water interface is only a fraction of a millimetre thick. Gases, liquids and solids pass between the air and the water, although the ocean does not supply much solid material to the air.

Chemicals dissolved in sea water can become incorporated into skeletons or sediments and, as a result, are removed from the ocean water. They are then returned to the land through uplifting or to the magma of the aesthenosphere through subduction. They are then available once more to be eroded or involved in hydrothermal activity.

This contribution and removal of material to and from the oceans is in balance: the oceans are said to be in a 'steady state'.

Right: *Close up, Dead Sea salt has a beauty all its own. The extensive formations found along the edges of the Dead Sea comprise billions of these intricately shaped crystals. Crystals form as a result of many natural processes. Another example is the formation of snow flakes, each flake being a single crystal. The component parts of a crystal are arranged in a precise pattern, occupying definite positions relative to one another.*

CYCLES

On the previous page, the oceans are said to be in a steady state, in which the rate of removal of chemicals from the water equals the rate of their addition. This rate depends intimately upon the various chemical and biological reactions that take place in the ocean water and in the sediment lining the sea floor.

'Bio-' chemicals

There are three principal kinds of chemicals in sea water. First, there are the so-called 'biolimiting' ones, which are used up quickly by plants as they grow and reproduce in the surface waters. They are called 'biolimiting' because if they are not replenished from the deep ocean, biological activity, such as plant growth and reproduction, ceases. Second, there are the 'biounlimiting' chemicals. These are not depleted in the surface waters because they play only a minor role in the various biological processes that occur there. Third, the 'biointermediate' chemicals are only partially used up and thus only partly limit plant growth and reproduction.

Of these, the biolimiting chemicals are the most intimately involved in biological cycles. They include nitrate, phospate and silicate. When animals and plants die, they sink to the ocean floor, and the animal or plant matter breaks down into its original components – nitrate, phosphate and so on. These chemicals then contribute to the nutrient reservoir which feeds the upwelling regions, e.g. along the Peruvian coast.

Sometimes the breakdown process is completed only once the material has reached the ocean floor. The released chemicals may then become incorporated into the sediment. Skeletal material takes longer to decay than softer tissue, hence its constituent chemicals go through a slower cycle.

Right: *These microscopic, single-celled organisms are called diatoms. They are plants, being one of the many kinds of phytoplankton. Unlike other unicellular plants, however, diatoms have walls impregnated with a silicon-based material, which often produces intricately sculptured surfaces. Although the shapes of diatoms are diverse, there are four main categories: pillbox – usually circular and sometimes in chains; filamentous – always in cylindrical chains; rod – needle-shaped and in chains or star-shaped clusters; branched – often bearing long spines or other projections. Some of these appear in the photograph. Diatoms can live on a variety of surfaces – rocks, sediments, other plants – as well as suspended in the water column. They are of crucial importance to life in the sea as, with other phytoplankton, they form the basis of the ocean food chain.*

The two-box model

To understand something of the processes that contribute to the nutrient and other cycles, it helps to envisage the ocean as two boxes. The upper box contains warm surface water, while the lower box, which is much larger, contains colder water. The region between the two boxes is known as the thermocline. To use this model, scientists make several assumptions.

First, it is assumed that chemicals are added to the ocean only by rivers. Other possible sources (e.g. hydrothermal activity) must be ignored. Second, it is assumed that dissolved chemicals are removed from the water in one of only two ways. Either they attach to falling particles which are deposited on the sea bed, or they are incorporated directly into the sea bed from the water. Third, it is assumed that the ocean is in a steady state, i.e. the rate at which chemicals enter it is exactly the same as the rate at which they leave it.

From these assumptions, it follows that whatever chemicals enter the ocean via the rivers are removed into the sediment in precisely the same quantity, since the overall amount in the boxes remains the same.

Chemicals introduced by the rivers into the upper box, then, are transferred to the lower box by downwelling water or by attaching to falling particles. Since the volume in each box cannot change, the volume of downwelling water must be balanced by an equal volume of upwelling water. When the particles reach the sediment, either the chemicals remain attached and are incorporated into the sea bed, or they are redissolved and recycled upwards via the upwelling water.

The water involved in the exchange between the two boxes each year is equivalent in volume to a layer about 6ft (2m) deep over the entire ocean surface.

On page 16, it is explained that water spills over the ridge between Greenland and the British Isles, then flows south in the western Atlantic Ocean. Falling particles carried by this current are joined by nutrients borne by cold water from the Antarctic. By means of deep circulation, this biologically important material is carried as far afield as the western Atlantic and the Indo-Pacific.

Right: *Chemicals trapped in the sediment may redissolve if the particles to which they are attached are disturbed. Others dissolve out of the sediment when they are buried and when oxygen binding them to the particles is used up by bacteria or other organisms on the sea floor.*

Right: ***Two-box model***

HOT SPRINGS IN THE SEA

In all the oceans, new sea floor is being thrown up in ridges by upwellings of lava from within the earth. Along these mid-ocean ridges are located springs of heated water. In 1977, on the Pacific Ocean Ridge near the Galapagos, water of 42–68°F (6–20°C) was found emerging at a depth of 8000ft (2500m) into the cooler (35°F/2°C) surrounding water. These springs were named 'warm-water' vents.

'Black smokers' and 'white smokers'

Vents spewing much hotter water have since been found along the East Pacific Rise and the Mid-Atlantic Ridge. The water is released through 'chimneys' up to 30ft (10m) in height. These are made up mostly of sulphides of iron, copper and zinc, laid down as the hot water reacts with the cold. Tiny sulphide particles also appear in a black smoke-like plume; hence the name 'black smoker'. The temperature of the water from these vents is around 662°F (350°C).

Other vents include the 'white smokers', with white plumes thought to be of barium sulphide particles.

All such vents, warm or hot, require certain basic geological conditions in order to exist. These conditions are similar to those associated with the land-based geysers of Iceland, New Zealand and North America. They include a permeable layer of rock which allows cold water to percolate downwards over a wide area into the earth's crust, a heat source below this layer, and several channels for the heated water to rise through and escape from the heat source. The percolation downwards occurs through the many cracks and crevices in the sea bed. In contrast, the upward flow is concentrated through only a few channels, which is why it escapes with such force.

New life forms

Strange animals, new to science, have been discovered around the vents, such as giant tube worms, blind crabs and shrimps. They use the chemical energy released during the reaction between the vent water and sea water. The more usual deep-sea animals do not go near the vents, presumably because the sulphides are toxic to them. Areas with accumulations of empty shells suggest vents once flowed there but have since ceased, leaving the populations to die.

Bacteria in the tissues of some vent animals

Left: *Note the sensors at the bottom of this photograph. The one on the left is a temperature probe. It is measuring the water temperature near the vent of this black smoker, one of many along the Pacific Ocean Ridge. Manoeuvring a submersible such as Alvin (see panel opposite) within just a few feet of the source of the hottest water in the ocean is a very skilful operation. If the vehicle approached too closely, the heat of the sulphide-rich water would melt the plastic portholes.*

Right: *The hydrothermal vent communities have been described as one of the great scientific discoveries of this century. They are animal communities that do not need sunlight, either directly or indirectly, in order to thrive, unlike nearly all other ocean life. Here, crabs can be seen crawling over a mussel bed in search of items of food. Some of the mussels have died and their shells have been picked clean.*

use the sulphide as food; in return, they supply food to the host vent animal. Bacteria able to live in high temperatures without oxygen have always been classified separately from other life forms. The discovery of such bacteria living in close proximity to higher-order creatures has prompted speculation that life itself may have originated in similar environments.

The animal assemblages of the Mid-Atlantic Ridge vents are dominated by shrimps, creatures not conspicuous around the Pacific vents and confined there to the warm-water outlets. The shrimps of the Atlantic vents live extremely close to the very hot chimneys, as many as 1500 per square yard (or square metre). They are not thought to act as host to bacteria in the way worms and mussels seem to. Instead, they gather food by mining sulphide from the chimneys themselves and then scraping off the bacteria living on the sulphide fragments.

Even more intriguing is the presence of clusters of light-sensitive cells on the backs of the shrimps. These clusters are not associated with a lens, so the shrimps cannot be seeing images in the conventional way. In any case, it is pitch black at such depth save for the occasional bioluminescent flash. First investigation suggests that black smokers are hot enough to emit a glow that can be detected by the shrimps, enabling them to find the chimneys but to avoid straying too close and being cooked.

Alvin

Many of the exciting discoveries about vents have been made by scientists on board 'Alvin'.

Alvin is a Deep Submergence Vehicle (DSV) named after the oceanographer Allyn Vine. It is quite small (26ft/8m long), with room for two or three people, and can travel at around 1 knot. It can descend to about 13,000ft (4000m), the cabin being inside a sphere of titanium capable of withstanding the enormous deep-ocean pressures. Observation is through four plastic portholes. The batteries and motors, attached to a framework outside the sphere, can be released in an emergency, allowing the sphere to rise to the surface. With three propellors, one aft and one each side, Alvin is very manoeuvrable. Lithium hydroxide scrubbers absorb the carbon dioxide breathed out by the crew, allowing nearly three days underwater. On board are depth gauges, a gyro compass, an echo sounder, an acoustic telephone (no wires to the surface), life support systems and a power pack; also scientific instruments, which vary according to the needs of the scientists – water and mud samplers, probes, cameras, etc. At the front of Alvin, two mechanical arms with pincers can perform remarkably delicate movements.

In July 1986, at almost its maximum working depth, Alvin observed the wreck of the SS Titanic, *which sank on the night of 14th April 1912 with the loss of nearly 1590 passengers and crew. Lying near one of the largest submarine canyons on the eastern North American continental shelf, the wreck had narrowly missed being broken up, or covered, by a massive turbidity current triggered by an earthquake in 1929. Debris from the ship was strewn over an area 5600ft by 2800ft (1700m by 875m). Recovery of the wreck, with its unique historical and social record, was considered to be out of the question.*

ORGANIC FOOD CYCLE

In the surface layers of the ocean, marine plants (particularly phytoplankton) thrive. They use water, carbon dioxide and the major nutrients – nitrate and phosphate – in a reaction driven by energy from sunlight. This process is known as photosynthesis. The manufacture of tissue by this means is called primary production.

By eating plants, herbivorous animals sustain themselves and are able to grow and reproduce. This growth is called secondary production. Herbivorous animals in turn become the food of carnivores, the growth and multiplication of which is called tertiary production. Carnivores are eaten by other carnivores, and so it goes on. Interlinking chains of this kind make up what is known as the food web.

Regeneration

Not all potential food is eaten to become food higher up its chain. Some production is lost through death, some burnt up as energy during life. After death, organic material breaks down and becomes available once more as food for the primary producers. The continuous process of breakdown and re-use is known as regeneration.

Sometimes the initial breakdown products cannot be used directly by plants, some intermediate action being needed to turn them into suitable raw materials. This is the job of bacteria, particularly plentiful on the sediments. As the bacteria break down the material further and release its constituent chemicals, they themselves grow and reproduce and are eaten by animals. Bacteria thus play a dual role – they produce food for plants and are actual food for animals. The nutrients they liberate in the deeper reaches of the ocean and on the ocean bottom have to be carried to the surface by upwelling currents before they can be used by the plants there.

Left: *The green turtle, seen here resting on coral rock next to a Gorgonia coral, is rather unusual among turtles as it is largely herbivorous. Most turtles include meat in their diets, such as fish. Green turtles feed mostly on sea grasses and other green plants, depending on what is available.*

Left: *The grey shark is a carnivore, feeding on fish, other sharks and offal. It is a predator at the top of a food chain, having few enemies and being unlikely to fall prey to another animal unless it is injured or until it grows too old or weak to fend for itself.*

Right: *These interesting shapes are single-celled organisms called radiolarians. They are animals, being one of the many kinds of zooplankton. They generally live at the ocean surface. After death they sink into the depths and are incorporated into one of the varieties of ooze lining the ocean floor.* *(See page 30.)*

Controls on plant growth

Various factors influence the intensity of plant activity. Plants contain a pigment called chlorophyll, which enables them to absorb light and use it as an energy source. Consequently the intensity of light (not just its presence) is a major factor. It must not be too bright or too dim, so the best position for plants may not be right at the water surface but a little distance down. Plants are able to build up energy reserves for when the light is not adequate for photosynthesis.

Temperature is another factor. The rate of photosynthesis increases up to a certain point as the temperature increases, after which it declines. Optimum photosynthesis takes place in different plants over different ranges of temperature.

Grazing by animals influences plant growth and survival. Phytoplankton may have a patchy distribution. While grazing by zooplankton depletes the phytoplankton in some areas, growth of new phytoplankton proceeds unhindered in others.

Another factor influencing plant productivity is the effectiveness with which nutrients are returned to the surface. In general, shallower, coastal areas are more productive than deeper areas further from land, nutrients having less distance to travel on their return to the surface.

Turbulence is a general term for various movements which cause different water layers to become mixed and therefore play a part in bringing nutrients to, and removing them from, the ocean surface.

Turbulence

There are several kinds of turbulence. One of these – convection – occurs when water cools, increases in density and sinks, being replaced by warmer, more buoyant water. Convection takes place continuously in the polar regions, mostly in winter in temperate parts, and hardly at all in the tropics.

Another kind of turbulence is seen when currents flow over an irregular sea bottom. The up and down movement can disturb the entire water column and cause mixing.

Internal waves, as high as 650ft (200m) in the deep ocean, are caused by wind blowing onshore over the continental shelf. The water layers bend under the influence of a strong wind and straighten when the wind relents. In this way, an oscillation can be set up and can be sufficiently violent to capsize the water layers; less dense water from near the surface is trapped beneath denser water from lower down. The less dense water then shoots back up to the surface.

Effect of the seasons

All these factors influencing plant productivity are themselves subject to seasonal variation. In temperate regions in winter, the ocean surface loses heat. This cooling causes convection, which, together with internal waves set up by the winds, brings nutrients to the surface. In spring, as the days lengthen, the light stimulates the growth and reproduction of phytoplankton. The winds die down and the nutrients begin to be used up. Zooplankton increase once the phytoplankton, their food source, become dense. As summer passes, the nutrients continue to be used up. As autumn develops, the water cools, the daylength decreases, and heavy feeding by zooplankton outstrips plant growth. There is some replenishment of nutrients by turbulence from autumn storms, but generally the plankton die off as winter sets in.

In polar regions, there are in effect only two seasons, one with light and one without. There is a burst of activity in the first of these.

In the tropics, stable conditions of warmth and light mean the water column is more rigidly layered (stratified). There is little upwelling and thus little return of nutrients to the surface, although changing wind patterns, e.g. monsoons, may cause sufficient turbulence to allow some nutrient replenishment.

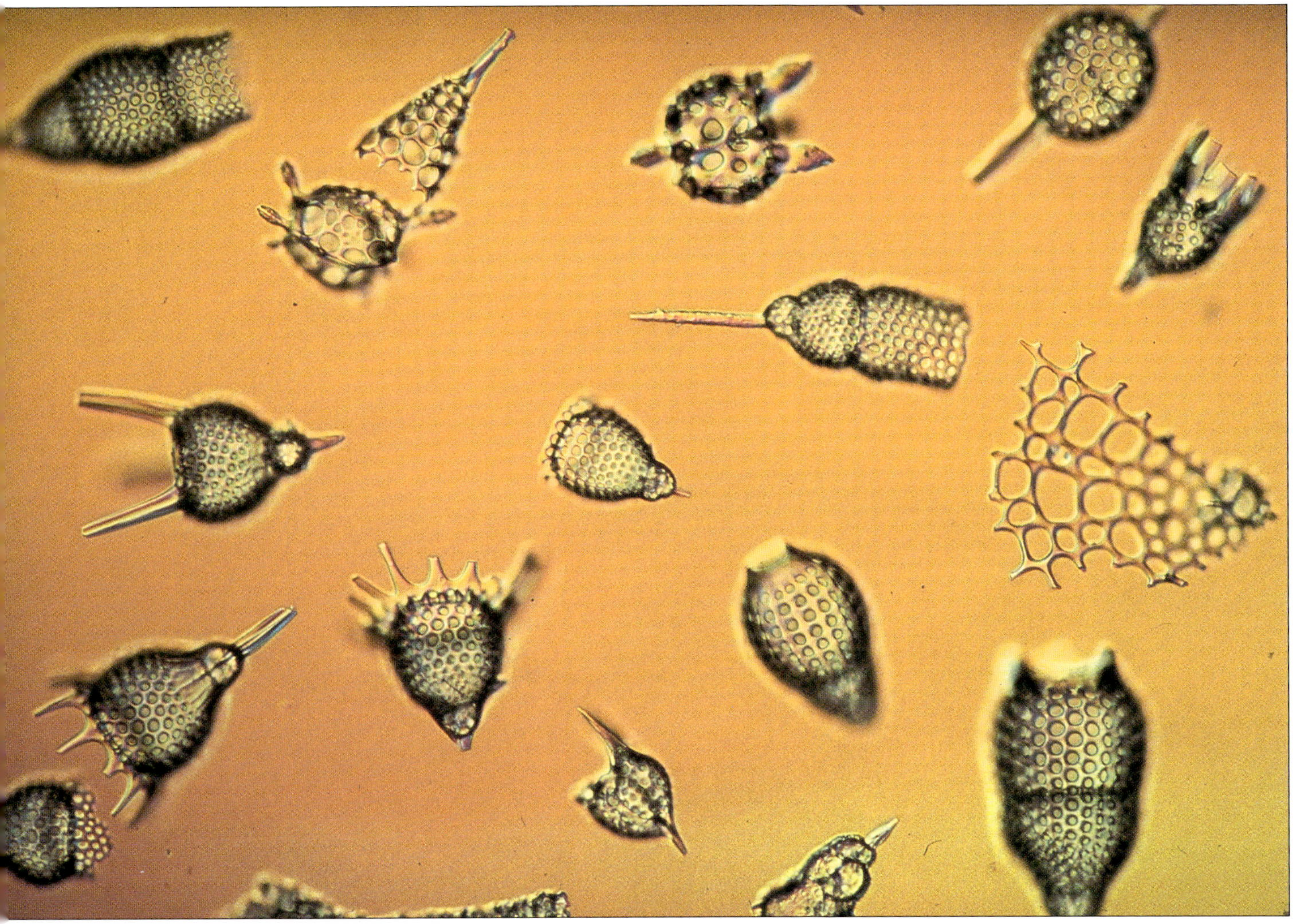

4·Sediments Around the Sea

EROSION AND DISTRIBUTION

Nearly all the sediments that line the oceans are derived from the erosion by weathering of rocks on land. Weathering is influenced by a number of factors, including the prevailing climate and the nature of the rock in question. It can be either mechanical or chemical.

Kinds of weathering

Mechanical weathering is the breaking of rock into fragments, a process sometimes accelerated by frost shattering. This occurs when water enters cracks in the rock and freezes. As it freezes, it expands and fractures the rock. After a number of thaws and freezes, the rock breaks. In very dry climates with daily extremes of high and low temperature, the alternate heating and cooling can have the same effect.

With chemical weathering, water passes over rock and breaks it down by reacting chemically with it.

Transport of sediment

The products of weathering – rock fragments (including boulders) and dissolved chemicals – are carried to the ocean principally by rivers. Wind, however, can carry dust particles, perhaps from deserts or volcanic ash deposits, while moving ice (glaciers) can transport fragments of all sizes. In the rivers, the fragments rub against each other and against the rocks they pass over. Both the fragments and the rocks of the river become smooth and rounded and may lose material by reacting chemically with the river water. Many millions of tons of sediment are delivered to the oceans every year.

The general seaward movement of sediment can be speeded up or slowed down by storms or droughts respectively. The building of dams across rivers, too, can almost totally prevent sediment reaching the sea. Two major rivers effected in this way are the Nile and the Colorado.

Sediments of the ocean floor

Sediments on the ocean floor are of three kinds. Detrital sediments are those derived from mechanical weathering and take the form of gravels, sands, silts and clays. Another kind includes those with a biological source, such as chalk from shell banks and coral reefs. The third kind is those that form through chemical reaction on the sea bed – manganese nodules and phosphate deposits are examples. (See page 37.)

Detrital sediments are found in greatest quantity on the continental shelf, where currents and wave action disturb and mix them. Further quantities settle on the continental slope and rise and in the ocean trenches. Turbidity currents and deep ocean currents carry yet further quantities onto the plains of the deep-ocean floor.

Deposits near land may contain a fair amount of organic matter, e.g. leaf, wood and skeletal fragments. They vary in coarseness, too, from boulders, through various grades of pebble, sand and gravel, to fine clay. Generally they are a mixture of several of these.

Most deep-ocean deposits are very fine and contain remnants of animals that once lived in the surface waters above. They are known collectively as oozes and are of several kinds.

First, there are calcareous deposits, i.e. deposits containing calcium carbonate. These are of three types: globigerina ooze, which covers most of the deep-ocean floor of the Indo-Pacific and Atlantic; pteropod ooze, which covers the floor of the subtropical Atlantic; and coccolith ooze, which coats the ocean floor beneath warm surface water. Second, there are siliceous deposits, based on silicon rather than calcium carbonate. These are of two types: diatom ooze, which appears as a belt around the Antarctic; and radiolarian ooze, which lies beneath the Indo-Pacific and Atlantic in the tropics.

Left: *In some parts of the world, wind carries considerable quantities of land soil to the ocean in the form of dust. This dust devil is in the Sonora Desert, Mexico.*

Right: *The most important agent by which rocks and soil are transported to the world's oceans is water, particularly if it is fast flowing. This dramatic shot is of the Sete Quedas on the Brazil–Paraguay border, plummeting over a hundred feet into the swirling water below. The passage of such enormous quantities of water through a restricted channel can be responsible for the erosion and transportation of many tonnes of sediment a day. The sediment carried by this river gives the water its rich muddy colour.*

SEAS

A sea is a partially enclosed marine area joined to an ocean. This definition embraces rather vast expanses of water such as the Gulf of Mexico, the Caribbean and the Mediterranean, but perhaps for most people a sea is something on the lesser scale of, say, the North Sea or the Black Sea. These two latter seas are actually quite different from each other. While the North Sea is relatively shallow and is termed a shelf sea, the Black Sea is quite deep and is known as a deep basin.

Shelf seas

A shelf sea has a number of features in common with that part of an ocean over a continental shelf. The movement of sediment is determined largely by the wind and tides. Onshore winds drive currents which run up against the coast, are deflected and run parallel to the coast until deflected again by, say, a headland. In this manner, currents tend to have a rather circular motion.

As on a continental shelf, the principal source of sediment in a shelf sea is the land. Sediment is carried almost entirely by rivers. Interestingly, the North Sea is not fed with substantial loads of sediment because the rivers that enter it have rather large estuaries and these trap much of the sediment. In contrast, the Yangtze River delivers substantial quantities of sediment to the Yellow Sea (similar in size to the North Sea), perhaps as much as 5–10 tonnes a year. The sediments on the bed of the North Sea were probably laid down during the release of glacier melt water. The glaciers carried coarse sands and gravels rather than the finer material generally transported by the rivers.

Deep basins

Extremes of temperature and salinity are features of these seas. One of the largest variations in average temperature, 65–68°F (18–20°C), has been recorded in the Black Sea. Hydrothermal circulation in the Red Sea, however, can raise the local water temperature to 132°F (56°C). Fresh water flowing into the Baltic Sea can reduce substantially the salinity of the sea water. The Black Sea receives water from three rivers – the Danube, Dnieper and Dniester – which can so dilute the surface water that its salt content is a mere 50 per cent of that normal for sea water.

There are two further characteristics of deep basin seas. One is turbidity currents, which carry accumulating sediment from the shallower to the deeper regions. The other results from the very shape of the basin itself.

The depth of the basin can restrict water circulation, resulting in the supply of oxygen to the deeper regions being cut off. At the bottom of the basin there is almost no oxygen and hence almost no animal life. The only living organisms known to exist on the sea bed are the specialised, microscopic sulphur bacteria.

In the oceans, too, oxygen levels can be reduced at depth. Some deep basins not depleted of oxygen at the bottom are nevertheless depleted locally around the side. This comes about when a deep basin connects with the adjacent ocean at the level at which the ocean water is low in oxygen.

Below: ***A shelf sea***

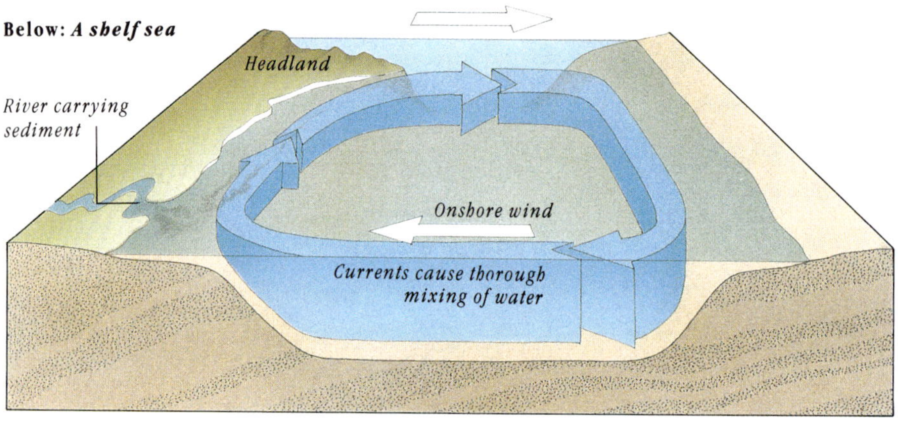

Below: ***A deep basin***

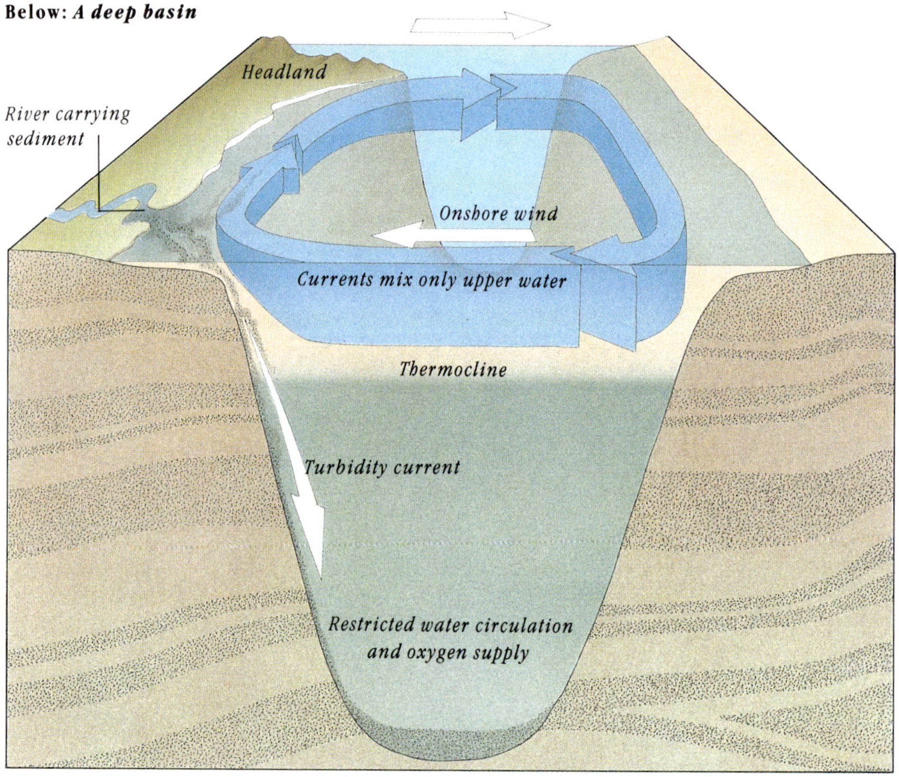

The life of an ocean

The formation of an ocean is extremely slow. Since the first maps were drawn (about 500 years ago), the Atlantic Ocean has widened by perhaps 50ft (15m).

There are a number of stages an ocean is thought to go through, from initial rift, to reaching its maximum dimension and to final closure. Although not everyone agrees, the East African Rift Valley may be an example of the first stage, the rifting of the continental mass. This stage is followed by the moving apart of the two sides of the rift and the accumulation of sediment from the two continental margins to form the shelf area. Examples may be the Red Sea (see photograph) and the Gulf of California.

As the continents continue to move apart, upwelling occurs between the plates, and the hot ridge gradually becomes distinct from the cooling and sinking ocean floor (as in the Atlantic Ocean). Destructive plate margins develop, and the spreading slows down or stops, perhaps because of new continental rifting. The Pacific Ocean is considered to be closing. The African plate is being subducted under the European plate, resulting in the demise of the Mediterranean Sea and the throwing up of new mountain ranges (e.g. the Alps and Pyrenees).

Finally all that is left is a scar where there was once an ocean. Scientists believe the Himalayas are such, still forming as a result of India moving towards Asia and thereby closing the ocean that once lay between them.

ESTUARIES

An estuary is where a river meets the sea. At the mouth of a river there is a gradient of salinity (saltiness) between the fresh water of the river and the saline (salty) water of the sea. This gradient fluctuates continuously with the state of the tide and varies, too, with the amount of fresh water coming down the river. The more fresh water there is, the more dilute, i.e. the less saline, is the water at the mouth of the estuary. Water of a saltiness between that of fresh water and that of sea water is called brackish water. In many estuaries there is also an irregular vertical gradient of salinity between the surface and the estuary bed, with the fresh water forming a floating layer above the denser salt water.

Chemistry of estuary water

Estuary water, however, is not a simple dilution of sea water. There are many subtle differences in chemical composition. The relative amounts of the various constituents of estuary, sea and river water differ widely between all three. These differences themselves vary with the seasons or even daily.

If the water column is stratified (or layered) because of, say, differences in salinity between sea water and fresh water, the lower strata (or layers) may become devoid of oxygen. This is especially common in summer.

Chemical substances that do not occur in great quantity, such as iron, silicon and phosphate, are often present in river water in much higher concentrations than in sea water. If the catchment that a river and its tributaries flow through and drain is a mining area, there may well be large amounts of manganese, copper or zinc in the water.

Rivers may also transport great numbers of particles suspended in the water. These particles release or bind onto metals in the water, thereby affecting the overall concentrations of the metals. Depending upon what material a river flows over, the acidity of the water may also vary. For instance, the presence of humic substances from peaty areas may make the water more acid, while the presence of limestone is likely to have the opposite effect.

Mudflats

Large amounts of silt may be deposited at a river mouth forming extensive mudflats. Some rivers deposit this silt in a fan shape (or delta) beneath the sea water. The Nile and Rhone have built up deltas which extend several miles out to sea. Areas in which there has been extensive deposition of mud under expanses of shallow water experience greater cooling and warming than the rest of the estuary. In cold periods, or during rains, cooler temperatures predominate because of the large outflow of cool fresh water. In warm periods there is an increase in temperature on account of heating by the sun and the lesser outflow of cool river water.

In the narrower parts of an estuary the tides produce powerful currents. These currents scour the estuary bed, particularly where there are large accumulations of silt. Wave action lessens with decreasing depth as friction between waves and the bed increases.

Salinity gradient in a river estuary

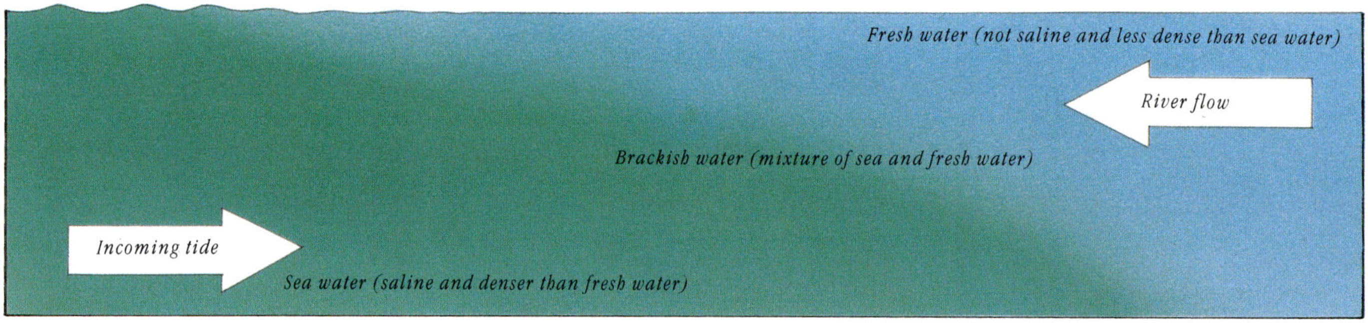

DELTAS

Large rivers carrying great volumes of sediment to the sea deposit their loads in huge fan-shaped formations called deltas. Sometimes a number of these formations together resemble a gigantic bird's foot: part of the delta of the Mississippi is an example. The sediments are mostly silts and clays rather than sands. Most of the world's major rivers have deltas: the Ganges, the Niger, the Mississippi, the Tigris–Euphrates, the Yellow River, the Nile and the Yukon. A delta may extend out to sea by as much as 30 miles (50km), with new sediment being deposited continuously along a 1000ft (300m) front. Under a delta the earth's crust may actually subside on account of the pressure from the overlying sediment. For instance, it is known that the Mississippi delta reaches a thickness of 6 miles (10km).

Formation of deltas

Wave action tends to disperse sediment along the shoreline as it begins to accumulate at the mouth of a river. Hence, for a delta to form two conditions must be fulfilled. First, the river must be carrying a massive volume of sediment; and second, there must be an indentation in the coastline in order to allow the delta to begin forming.

If the water is very shallow where a delta is beginning to form, marshland may well develop as the sediment piles up and plant seeds, transported by the wind, land and germinate.

Growth of deltas

As a delta builds up and extends into the deeper water of the ocean, its advance slows because strong wave action and tidal currents begin to distribute the accumulating sediments more evenly. With continuing growth, however, pressure on the continental shelf from the sheer weight of sediment can cause the shelf in front of the delta to bulge outwards. Two examples of this can be seen in the vicinity of the Niger and Nile deltas. In other cases the continental shelf does not give way, and a delta builds out over the shelf without effect, as in the case of the Mississippi delta. Some fingers of this delta extend so far that their sediments actually accumulate on the continental slope. In both cases, though, deltas are able to extend only so far, where the general water depth is quite shallow, thus reducing wave and tidal scouring action.

Where a delta is extending onto a continental shelf, a curious occurrence is the possible formation of small hills. These hills are called mud lumps if they are very small and diapirs if they are larger. They form as a result of squeezing between the accumulating sediments, pressing down, and less dense sediments underneath, pressing up. They are quite common in the Gulf of Mexico and may be found to overlie oil deposits. For example, oil is often found under diapirs off Texas and Louisiana.

Left: *This satellite view is of the Colorado River delta at the edge of the Gulf of California. The river surges through great canyons on its way to the sea, eroding the rock over which it flows and becoming laden with huge amounts of sediment. Much of this sediment is deposited on the delta. Damming of rivers such as the Colorado blocks the passage of a lot of sediment and therefore slows the growth of deltas.*

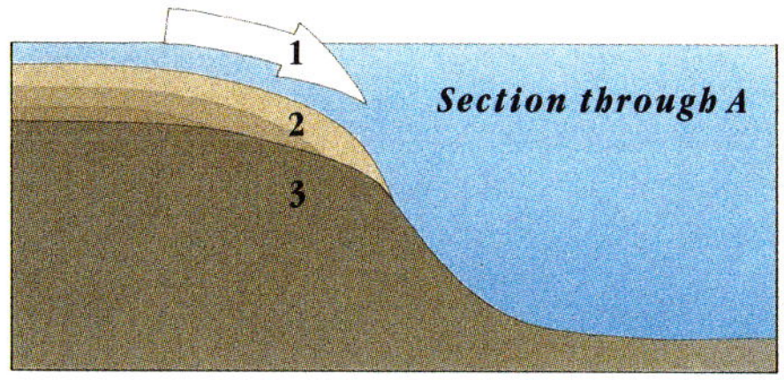

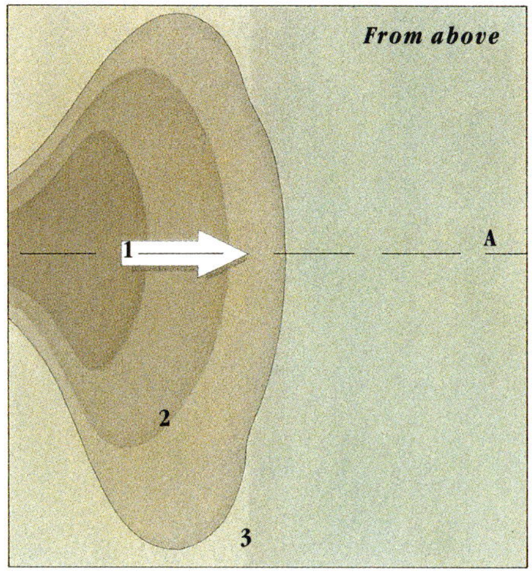

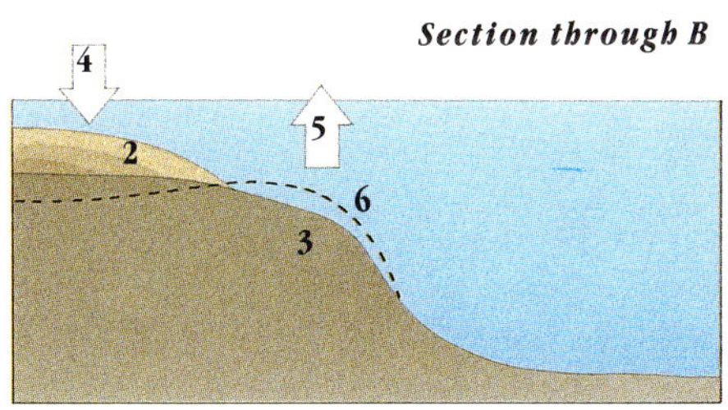

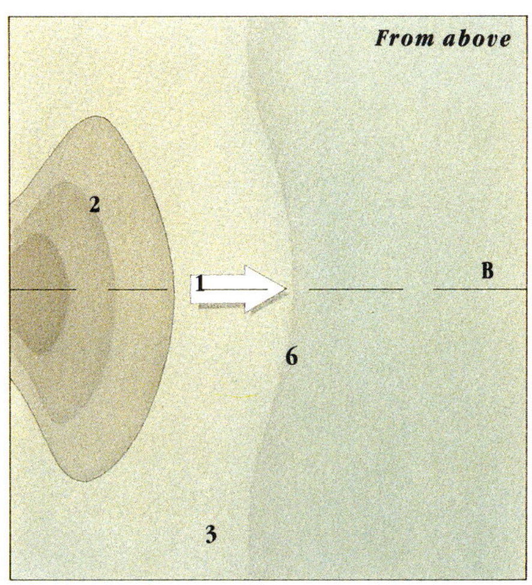

Left: *The weight of some deltas causes the continental shelf to bulge, much as an inflated balloon does when it is squeezed, i.e. upwards and outwards.*

1 *Forward growth of delta*
2 *Accumulating layers of sediment*
3 *Continental shelf*
4 *Downward pressure*
5 *Movement of continental shelf*
6 *Change in shape of continental shelf*

Above: *Some deltas extend over the edge of the continental shelf without effect.*

1 *Forward growth of delta*
2 *Accumulating layers of sediment*
3 *Continental shelf*

TURBIDITY CURRENTS

Sediment that has accumulated on the upper part of a continental slope may move in varying amounts to a lower part or even onto the abyssal plain. Movements are termed slides, slumps, debris flows or turbidity currents according to the degree of change the sediment that is moved undergoes. For instance, slides and slumps are simply shifts in position of material, perhaps because of earthquake activity. These relatively slight movements may involve material hundreds of metres thick and thousands wide. Debris flows cause greater disruption to the sediment that is carried and are responsible for the movement of vast quantities of material from one part of a slope to another.

Turbidity currents can completely alter the character of the moved sediment, and can be caused in a number of ways. Strong onshore winds, wave action or earthquakes can disturb sediment, which thereby becomes suspended in the water. Once sufficiently laden with sediment, the water flows down the continental slope. This flowing action has enough force to cut canyons in the slope, perhaps up to 1000ft (300m) deep. As turbidity currents emerge from such submarine canyons, they deposit to form huge fan-shaped areas of sediment. These fans are important contributors to the upper part of the continental shelf.

Turbidity currents also deposit sediment fans as far from their source as the abyssal plains, sometimes transporting sand onto these expanses of mud. They can carry material ranging from fine, dust-sized particles to pea-sized fragments.

Speeds of flow

During the Grand Banks earthquake in 1929, the submarine telephone lines that are routed through the region were sequentially broken as a massive turbidity current swept across them. Calculations using the times of breakage and the known distances between the lines suggest speeds of flow between 17 and 60mph (27 and 96km/hr). Such was the carrying capacity of this extremely powerful current that material is known to have been transported and spread more than 300 miles (500km) from its original location.

A turbidity current may not be contained solely within the canyon it scours out. It may spread out over a broad front, with fingers reaching forward at different speeds according partly to the shape of the terrain they are travelling over.

A turbidity current has a number of parts – the head, the neck and the body. These separate sections can travel at different speeds according to the loads of sediment they are carrying and to their heights. Scientists have calculated that the front region of a turbidity current that is carrying a large amount of very fine mud could be hundreds of metres high when it begins to move, and could progress, in the early stages, at speeds of around 50mph (80km/hr). As the gradient of the terrain levels out, the current slows down and the sediment begins to settle.

The settling sediments are deposited in sequence according to the size of the individual particles. The larger particles settle out first, the finest last. The latter, therefore, are found on top of a deposit. The sequential layers of a deposit are known as a turbidite sequence.

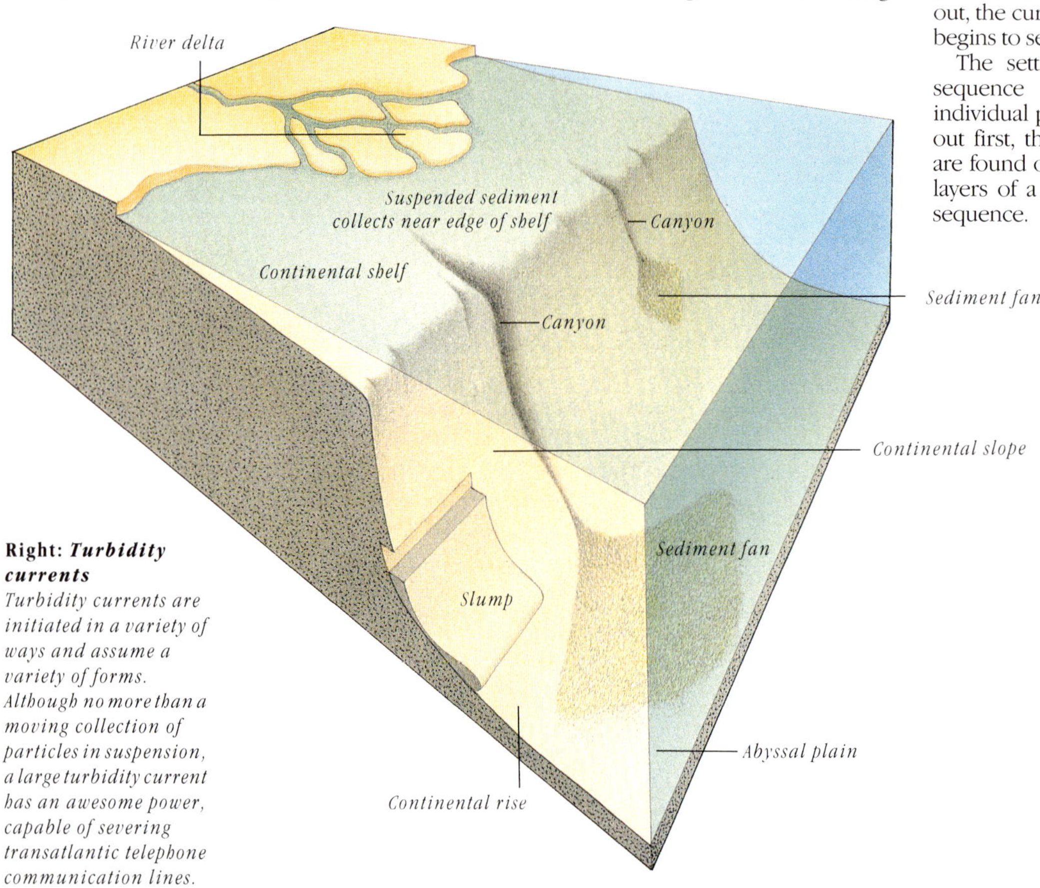

Right: *Turbidity currents*
Turbidity currents are initiated in a variety of ways and assume a variety of forms. Although no more than a moving collection of particles in suspension, a large turbidity current has an awesome power, capable of severing transatlantic telephone communication lines.

Right: *This manganese nodule, which comes from the Pacific Ocean, has been split open to reveal its internal structure. Note the darker, outer coating. This is an oxidised layer, where the material of the outside of the nodule has reacted chemically with oxygen in the sea water.*

Far right: *This field of manganese nodules is on the floor of the Pacific Ocean, at a depth of 16,000ft (4900m). Taking photographs of this kind is much easier than physically collecting nodules.*

MINERALS

Minerals are inorganic substances, such as metals, that occur naturally. They have a specific composition and are often found in large accumulations. Sea water itself contains many different kinds of metals, but these need to be deposited in a more concentrated form, e.g. as metal ore, before they are recovered commercially. There are huge reserves of minerals in the oceans formed through geological time, including phosphate deposits and manganese nodules, found in some sea-floor sediments. Oil, which is organic in origin but sometimes referred to as a mineral, forms under the sea bed (see pages 48–9), and so does gas. All these substances are forming today, some in the deep ocean and others in the shallow seas around our coastlines.

Phosphate deposits

Phosphates are a complex of chalk, fluoride and phosphate and accumulate on the continental shelves in the form of football-sized pellets or nodules. They appear in a number of shades of colour, ranging from light cream to black. Accumulations are found in the regions of the world where cool waters rich in nutrients are rising up (upwelling) quite close to land from the deeper parts of the ocean. The nutrients are derived from the decomposition of animal and plant material (e.g. plankton) and include phosphate.

While most phosphate deposits seem to have formed some time ago, there may be areas in which phosphate formation continues to take place today. Off south-west Africa and Peru, where there is rich upwelling water supporting substantial fisheries, it is thought that there is insufficient time for the rain of animal and plant remains to decompose fully before it reaches the deep-sea sediments. These partly decomposed remains are finally broken down in the sediments themselves. Through a series of poorly understood reactions, the breakdown products contribute to the accumulations of phosphate.

Manganese nodules

Manganese nodules occur in deep and shallow water. They are found lying on or just below the surface of the sea bed. They can appear as rounded structures the size of a golf ball or as slabs that cover several square metres and weigh over a tonne. Sometimes they encrust other rocks on the sea floor.

The deep- and shallow-water varieties differ in the rate at which they form. The shallow-water nodules form very rapidly, growing at up to one millimetre per year, whereas the deep-water variety grow at about one to five millimetres per million years.

Another major difference is in chemical composition. Copper and nickel accumulate in the deep-water nodules as they grow.

Exploitation

Phosphate deposits and manganese nodules are of sufficient quantity offshore to make their future collection commercially viable. To date, though, sources on land have been plentiful. Also, international legislation has yet to resolve the question of who owns many marine deposits and this, together with the technical difficulty of recovering them, has resulted in minimal exploitation so far.

5·ECOLOGY OF THE SEA

ESTUARIES

The river estuary is a very dynamic environment. Only a restricted range of animals and plants can cope with its rapidly altering conditions. However, there is an advantage in this. For those species that can survive, there is less competition from others for food and space. With less competition, species often thrive in high numbers.

Adaptations to estuary life

The moving water itself imposes problems on those animals that need to stay in a certain position in the estuary. There is a danger of being carried by the tide to water of too high or low a salinity - downstream by the outflowing, or ebbing, tide, or upstream by the rising, or flooding, tide. Specific behavioural responses to the changing tide have thus evolved - some animals swim on the flood while others sink to the bed on the ebb. Such adaptation to a changing environment is not only a feature of adult animals. For instance, young free-swimming stages of oysters settle on the bottom if the salinity falls too low.

Tolerance to changes in salinity and temperature determine how far marine animals venture upstream. The extent to which freshwater animals penetrate downstream depends upon the average freshwater flow and the availability of a suitable place to live. Some fish migrate landwards during the warmer months to feed on rich estuary sediments. Birds such as dunlin, oystercatchers and a variety of plovers, sandpipers, ducks and geese arrive in their hundreds, sometimes thousands, to feed on the wide mudflats - especially in winter, when food can be scarce.

Variation in tide and flow

Some estuaries have a sand bar across the mouth, which tends to reduce wave action. Where there is great seasonal variation in the flow of a river, an estuary mouth may close during the dry season. Some estuaries in southern Africa, for example, where the tidal range is generally limited, experience considerable wave action. The waves quickly throw up sand bars which close off the rivers. The enclosed lagoons so formed may gradually become quite fresh. In the wet season the river flow keeps the estuaries open to the sea.

Where there is a great tidal range, the tides sweep in and out of the estuary, and as the rising tide meets the fresh water, there may be extensive deposition of mud. This mud may remain bare or it may become colonised by a variety of plants to form a saltmarsh. (See page 39.)

Food supply and distribution

The amount of light that can penetrate the water of an estuary depends upon the quantity of material suspended in the water. The small microscopic plants called phytoplankton only grow where there is plenty of light, usually only near the surface of the water. These small plants generally form the basis of the food supply in an estuary. If, however, the water of an estuary is very turbid (muddy), the food produced by a saltmarsh may play a much more important role.

The distribution of mobile animal species, such as fish, is determined mostly by salinity, with other factors, such as food supply, superimposed on this. For more static animals, distribution is influenced primarily by the particle size, or the degree of coarseness, of the mud or sand in which they live; superimposed on this factor are others, such as salinity and water movement. Plant distributions are consequent in the first place on the amount of light available, and only secondarily on such factors as salinity.

PLANTS OF THE OCEAN MARGIN

Along a sheltered shoreline, of an inlet or estuary perhaps, water currents tend to lessen. As they do so, the silt and mud they are carrying settle and form deposits. These deposits gradually accumulate until, as the tide rises and falls, they remain emersed (above the water) for longer and longer periods of time. With this increased exposure to air comes an increasing attraction of the area to vegetation of a terrestrial (land-based) origin.

There are three main kinds of vegetation that favour this muddy, salty environment – saltmarsh plants, mangrove trees and sea grasses. Saltmarsh plants consist of grasses, herbs and dwarf shrubs. Mangroves comprise a range of species of large shrubs and trees. Sea grasses consist only of grass species.

Conditions for growth

Saltmarsh plants prefer cool, dryish conditions. They grow in temperate regions, particularly along the margins of estuaries. They do not like to be covered with sea water for extended periods. Mangrove trees, on the other hand, prefer areas subjected to extensive inundation – their roots are nearly always underwater – and occur in the tropics. Sea grasses grow worldwide and are always found underwater. Saltmarsh plants and mangroves always occur in the intertidal zone and on occasion are found along the same stretch of coast.

Saltmarshes and mangroves

The presence of saltmarsh and mangrove plants encourages additional deposition of sediment because the root systems of the plants serve to reduce the water currents still further. This sediment trapping gradually raises the level of a marsh or mangrove, allowing species that are less tolerant of submergence or salty conditions to gain a foothold and survive. These new additions to the saltmarsh or mangrove change the environment still more, encouraging further plant varieties to become established in succession.

Because the development of the marsh or mangrove depends on the kinds of plant species that are present, it takes place irregularly and is heavily influenced by local conditions. There are generally a lot of creeks through which the sea water rises and falls. These creeks are virtually marine and therefore allow the marsh or mangrove environment to be visited by marine species. They also act as pathways to and from the sea for those animals that establish themselves in the developing habitats.

Along with the sediment, quantities of nutrients are also trapped, providing a rich source of food. Shelter from extreme water movement and access to plenty of food make the saltmarsh and mangrove habitats highly attractive to terrestrial and marine fauna.

Sea grasses

Sea grasses are found almost entirely below the level of low water in depths varying from a couple of feet (less than a metre) to several times that. They can form extremely dense areas of cover, which have been likened to terrestrial meadows. Only a few animals (fish, turtles, sirenians and sea urchins) feed directly on the sea grass leaves, which are largely indigestible. Most animals that live among or visit the sea grasses feed on decomposing leaves or on those so feeding.

Sea-grass beds play host to a wide range of animals and other plants, and it is this, combined with the shelter afforded by the grasses, that makes them an ideal nursery for fish and shrimps.

Below left: *Creeks of this kind often cut deep into a saltmarsh. Sometimes they dry out as the tide recedes, sometimes sufficient water remains to allow the passage of marine animals into the inner reaches of the marsh.*

Below right: *Sea grasses grow in quite shallow water and provide shelter and food for many marine animals. Lurking among the leaves of this 'meadow' will be fish, crabs, sea urchins, sea cucumbers and shrimps.*

Left: *This mangrove scene in Australia features one of the principal mangrove tree species of the genus* Rhizophora. *Note the aerial roots hanging down from the ends of some of the branches. These roots will continue to grow until they reach the surface of the mud. Living among the tangle of a mangrove is a wide variety of creatures, including crabs and frogs.*

ROCKY SHORES

A rocky shore is a meeting place for terrestrial and marine animals and plants. The constantly changing tidal level creates an environment which makes particular demands on its inhabitants.

Zonation

Probably the first thing that a visitor to a rocky shore notices is the presence of distinct areas or bands running along it. These bands appear as light or dark strips. The upper one is often a collection of rotting seaweed – the strand line or high-water mark of the last tide. Further bands are a feature of zonation. Zonation represents a sequential change in the distribution of animals and plants from the highest part of the shore to the lowest.

The zonation that is picked out on a particular shore is a reflection of the interaction between the terrestrial and marine animals and plants that live there. What determines the end result of that interaction and, in large measure, the particular zonation of that shore is an array of interplaying factors.

Causes of zonation

The key factors are the tolerance of animals and plants to submergence and drying out, and the amount of wave action they can withstand.

Every part of a shore is covered and uncovered by the tide twice each day. The higher up the shore, the longer the period of exposure by the tide. Conversely, the tide uncovers and re-covers the lower shore much more quickly. Those animals and plants that do not like to be exposed for long periods tend to be found low down the shore, while those that are able to tolerate long periods of exposure, and the drying out that comes with that exposure, are found much higher up.

Most animals and plants found on a shore come from the sea. Sea spray extends the distance up the shore at which they are able to survive. The very top of the shore is where land animals and plants tend to live. They have to be able to tolerate sea spray and occasional wave action during stormy weather.

Zonation really involves those animals and plants that are fixed and cannot move. When the tide has covered a shore, various animals not normally seen on the exposed shore, particularly fish, move in to feed. Similarly, when the shore is exposed after the tide has receded, rats and birds visit, looking for food.

In addition to tolerance of submergence and wave action, there are other factors that determine what lives where and when. These are the forces of competition – for space and for food. In order to compete successfully for these two commodities, a species must outperform others in a number of areas, such as growth rate, the effectiveness of aggressive behaviour, and feeding efficiency (in this case, when the tide is covering the shore).

Animals that are fixed in one place (sedentary) need to occupy the right site if they are to survive, and their home location is carefully selected while they are in their younger, floating stages in the plankton. The distribution of mobile animals on the shore, such as crabs, depends on their ability to remove themselves from the causes of stress, i.e. particular environmental factors. For instance, crevices may offer protection from the pounding of waves.

Rocky shores around the globe reveal similar patterns of zonation. The relative importance of the key factors involved may vary, but the principles remain the same. For instance, in polar regions freezing and scraping by ice are important; the latter is the equivalent of wave action. In the tropics, after the tide has receded it is tolerance of high air temperatures and intense light conditions that determines primarily what lives where on a rocky shore.

The zoning of plants reflects their ability to withstand drying out when uncovered, buffeting from waves and from material thrown up by waves, and the grazing and browsing activities of shore animals.

Right: *This photograph of a headland on the coast of Wales illustrates one of the principal features of a rocky shore – zonation. Note contrasting light and dark areas. The dark band along the water's edge is seaweed, the lighter band higher up the shore is rocks encrusted with barnacles, and the dark band still higher is the debris along the strand line. Barnacle-covered rocks and pools can be seen in the foreground.*

KELP FORESTS

Kelp forests lie below the level of low water. They are sometimes visible when the lowest part of a shore is exposed during the spring tides. Kelp forests are the natural extension of rocky shores. They can be considered, in some respects, to be the temperate equivalent of tropical coral reefs.

The kelp plants

The kelp forest derives its name from the plants that dominate the underwater scenery – the kelp. These are large seaweeds that can be many metres in length. They provide a major habitat for smaller plant species and hundreds of different kinds of animals, including fish, crabs, shrimps, starfish and sea urchins.

The kelp plant consists of the holdfast, the stipe and the fronds, which are the equivalents, respectively, of a root, a stem and leaves. The holdfast is really just an attachment device and does not transport nutrients as do the roots of land plants. The fronds sweep back and forth with the movement of the tide and currents. As they do so, they sweep the rock surfaces and may dislodge animals. This sweeping action also keeps the surfaces clear of sediment, which serves to encourage other animals and plants to become established (e.g. sea anemones, sponges, seaweeds).

Distribution of plants

As light penetrates the water, it is absorbed according to how much sediment is suspended in the water. Some colours, such as blue, penetrate much more deeply than others. As the water becomes deeper, plants tend to predominate on the rocks according to their light preferences. Wave action is also important, some plants being more resistant to it than others.

While light and wave action are important in determining where plants grow, there are other, biological controls. Young kelp plants need clean rock surfaces on which to grow. Once established on a rock surface, the next control is the level of grazing pressure from a variety of marine animals. Grazing by sea urchins, for example, is a major control on kelp populations (and could, in fact, be considered equivalent to the grazing by the Crown of Thorns starfish on coral reefs. (See page 43.))

Along coasts of the Pacific Ocean, feeding by sea otter populations in turn keeps down the numbers of kelp grazers.

Right: *This view of a rocky shore was taken at very low water (on a spring tide). Kelp, which is clearly visible all along the shore, can tolerate exposure to air for short periods of time. In the foreground it is possible to discern the three primary parts of a kelp plant – the frond(leaf), stipe(stem) and holdfast (root).*

Below: *This Californian sea otter is wrapping up in a length of kelp for the night. During the day these charming creatures can be seen diving to collect tasty morsels from the sea bed, such as abalone (a kind of mollusc with a shell lined with mother-of-pearl).*

CORAL REEFS

Coral reefs are built up by millions of tiny animals (coral polyps) and plants (coralline algae). Their skeletons are made of calcium carbonate, the main component of limestone, and these, after death, become cemented together to make a reef. It can take thousands of years for a reef several metres thick to form.

Coral growth and reef formations

The successful formation of a reef is due mostly to the action of microscopic, single-celled plants called zooxanthellae. These live in the tissue cells of the polyp. Like other green plants, they use sunlight, carbon dioxide and nutrients to make food and grow. They obtain carbon dioxide from the coral polyp, and nutrients from the surrounding water and possibly also from the polyp. In return, they pass material back to the polyp. During the laying down of calcium carbonate, the polyps release the carbon dioxide used by the zooxanthellae. Their use of carbon dioxide is thought to enhance the production of more calcium carbonate.

Three formations of reefs are commonly found, although intermediate forms also occur — fringing reefs, barrier reefs and atolls. They are probably related in their development. Fringing reefs form close inshore on rocky coastlines or around a volcano that is gradually sinking into the sea. As the volcano sinks and the coral grows upwards, a channel develops between the two: a barrier reef is forming. When the volcano has sunk, only a ring of coral remains: an atoll has formed. This simple theory does not explain all reef development, but is a good starting point.

Coral variety and zonation

Corals occur in the Atlantic, Indian and Pacific Oceans. No species are common to both the Atlantic and the Indo-Pacific regions, yet a number from each are clearly related, pointing to a common ancestry. Fossil evidence suggests the same. This notion supports the generally held belief that there was just one ocean in former times. Since corals cannot survive in the relatively cold water currents which flow round the southern tips of America and Africa, they cannot pass from one ocean to another. Because of this barrier to migration, the Atlantic corals and the Indo-Pacific corals have evolved into separate species.

Corals grow best where there is sunlight, a stable temperature of about 68°F (20°C), plenty of oxygen and a good food supply. These conditions are usually found from mid-tide level down to about 130ft (40m), between the Tropics of Cancer and Capricorn. Corals do not like water which is too salty, too warm or too cool. They do not like being covered in silt or washed over by fresh water, and they cannot grow too deep, in weak light.

A reef includes many kinds of corals, often of different colours, and is the marine equivalent of a tropical rainforest in terms of the variety of animal life it supports. There are hundreds of kinds of fish, crabs, shrimps, crayfish, sea urchins, starfish, sea cucumbers, sea fans, sponges, sea anemones and worms, all occupying individual habitats.

Different corals, and hence different animals, flourish according to the depth and the amount of water movement. This arrangement is known as zonation. Corals do

Above: *Polyps of the coral* Tubastrea, *some open, others closed. Their food-catching tentacles spread out at night to seize passing zooplankton.*

Right: *The rounded shapes of the massive but intricately patterned brain coral lie just in front of a tall, hand-like sea fan. Both species contribute to the diversity of form in this Bahamian reef scene. The sea fan is oriented across the current, which flows through the mesh-like framework. As the water passes through the fan, minute particles of food are strained out by the colonies of animals that make up its structure.*

not grow much right inshore when backed by a sandy beach, in the area known as the reef flat; it is too silty here, and corals in this zone are frequently exposed at low tide. Further out, in deeper water with less wave action, small, branched corals grow quickly in the bright light. Deeper still, plate-like corals abound, their shape allowing them to capture more of the weaker light.

Corals grow at different rates according to their position on the reef. The branching forms grow relatively quickly, while others, described as 'massive', are slow growers. These can protect themselves from being overgrown by the branched variety by casting filaments towards any branches that come too close. The filaments digest the branch tissue, thus preventing it from growing.

Reef management

Coral reefs around the world today are under threat. They are a valuable resource and should not be over-exploited. Local communities fish on them. Companies mine them for limestone, thereby killing animals that shelter or feed there and depriving many species of their natural habitat. Tourists tread areas of inshore reef flat, breaking off masses of branches which can take years to re-grow. Scuba divers, if they are not careful, do the same underwater. Oil exploration, the building of coastal holiday resorts and hotels, and the souvenir trade all take their toll.

Carefully managed, coral reefs have a lot to offer, and that careful management is the challenge of today, not tomorrow. Sadly, that challenge is not being met in some places.

The Crown of Thorns starfish

The Crown of Thorns is a big starfish covered in thousands of toxic spines up to 2in (5cm) long. It can travel as fast as 65ft (20m) per hour, though its more usual speed is 3–12ft (1–4m) per hour. It may appear on a reef in its thousands, then depart just as suddenly, having eaten all the living coral and leaving behind just white limestone.

Such outbreaks were noticed on the Great Barrier Reef of Australia around 1962, and now more than a quarter of the reef is affected. Fast-growing corals can recover over five to fifteen years, but slow growers take much longer. It is still not clear whether infestations of the starfish are natural events or triggered by the activities of Man, such as overfishing, the collection of triton shells (major predators of the starfish) or pollution. Outbreaks have been traced in the fossil record as far back as 8000 years, suggesting to some a combination of natural and man-induced factors.

THE DEEP OCEAN

The greater part of the ocean is deep ocean. At first glance, this might seem an inhospitable environment and unlikely to support life. It is certainly very different from the warm, sunlit surface, but in fact is closely connected to this.

Light, temperature and salinity

When sunlight passes through the ocean surface, the individual colours of the spectrum are absorbed by particles in the water and the water itself. At just a few centimetres deep, the red end of the spectrum begins to be absorbed. A few tens of metres deep, green and blue are the only colours still present. Blue light might penetrate down to over 3000ft (1000m) in the clearest of ocean waters; however, this incredibly faint light would be undetectable to the naked human eye. Since most of the ocean lies below this depth, it is largely pitch black to humans.

The temperature falls rapidly with increasing depth until it is extremely cold, although there are local elevations of temperature, such as are found near hydrothermal vents. (See page 26.) The salt concentration can fluctuate at the surface, where rainfall or freshwater from rivers dilutes local areas. The larger part of the deep ocean, however, has a constant salt content.

The deep ocean, then, is characterised by a constant cold temperature, a constant salt content and an absence of light. For a long time, biologists believed the deep ocean was a lifeless desert.

Life in the depths

Following the transglobal expedition of HMS *Challenger* in the 1870s, the myth of a lifeless desert was dispelled. With trawls and dredges, the expedition's scientists scooped up an enormous variety of animals. These were caught at all depths, from mid water down to the sea floor and even into the deep ocean trenches. The diversity of animals and their discovery in most parts of the ocean prompted the question as to what they were eating. Research in the 1970s demonstrated that there is a continuous rain of food particles from the sunlit surface zone. The majority of ocean currents flow through the deep ocean; hence, even the seasonal changes evident in the upper ocean are felt in the deep. The deep ocean is not void of life; it is home for the most highly adapted animals of the oceans and for some of the oldest. Species previously considered to have died out centuries ago still thrive there.

Many species that live in the deep ocean (though not on the ocean floor) rise to the surface during the hours of darkness and descend again as daylight approaches. The main stimulus for this so-called vertical migration is believed to be the need of smaller species to feed on the plankton near the surface. These smaller animals are followed by larger predators, and these by larger still. Animals may also rise to breed, their eggs and subsequent young stages contributing to the plankton.

Scavengers and predators

Because most of the deep ocean is dark, plants cannot survive there; hence there is a marked absence of plant-eating animals or herbivores in the ocean depths. The animals that do live in the deep ocean are nearly all scavengers and predators. Scavengers live on any animal or plant matter sinking through the water column. Consequently, the deeper a scavenger lives, the less food it is likely to come across, animals above having eaten more of the available supply.

Predators, mostly fish, have developed a number of interesting adaptations in order to cope with the rigours of hunting in the depths. They have particularly large, often extensible, mouths, allowing them to seize an animal to eat almost irrespective of its size. Such ability is vital since there may be a long time between meals. Accompanying the large mouths are sets of strong teeth and extensible stomachs, and fish in the mid-water regions may have especially large eyes.

Perhaps the most impressive development is that of the lure, used by many species to tempt prey within reach of their huge mouths. These lures contain light-producing organs, the light usually coming from luminescent bacteria within the organ. Luminescent lures attract small fish, themselves searching for food, in an otherwise pitch black environment.

As scientists continue to search the dark waters of the deep ocean and to observe the life-forms to be found there, new wonders are almost certain to come to light.

ECOLOGY OF THE OCEAN FLOOR

Animals that live on the various soft muds, or oozes, that coat the ocean floor must be specially adapted if they are not to sink into them. Adaptations include a flattened form, spines, stalks, and long legs with hairs. Another feature is the development of gigantism – while the vast majority of animals are quite small, a few species have gone in for spectacular size. This is believed to be the result of a scarcity of food and consequent slow growth.

Shrimps, crabs, sea urchins, snails, worms and starfish are all represented in the fauna of the ocean floor. Some live on the sediment, others burrow into it. They feed on particles and clumps of organic matter that descend from the upper ocean. If large clumps settle on the sea floor, those animals that are mobile, such as shrimps and starfish, gradually home in on them. Fish arrive later, attracted by particles released by the feeding activity of the animals that got there first. Sedentary animals (those fixed in one place), such as sponges and tube worms, feed on particles that settle on them.

The life in the upper, sunlit part of the ocean is the key to the survival of the deep-ocean and ocean-floor animals. Without the continuous rain of particles and descent of dead animals and plants, there would be insufficient food available. Even those animals believed to take in dissolved substances rely on the generation of these in the upper ocean. Perhaps the only animal communities truly independent of the ocean surface are the hydrothermal vent communities.

Left: *A deep-sea angler fish waves its bioluminescent lure temptingly in the dark. Note its huge mouth and fierce-looking teeth. Opportunities to catch food are not frequent, so when the chance to seize a fish presents itself, it must not be lost. The lower jaw can articulate so that prey almost as large as the angler itself can be swallowed. Similarly, the stomach can extend to accommodate large prey.*

Above: *This cleaner shrimp lives among the waving tentacles of anemones and feeds on discarded crumbs of food. Shrimps are scavengers and are also found on the soft sediments of the ocean floor.*

Right: *This starfish is a predator, and the clam feeds on particles of debris. Both animals have deep-water cousins that feed in the same way.*

THE ECOSYSTEM

It should now be apparent that ocean geology, physics, chemistry, sediments and ecology are interlinked. The ocean has to be considered as a functional whole; that is to say, change in one aspect of the ocean environment may influence one or more other aspects. Such influence may take effect on a large scale, as in the linking of winds, currents, nutrient supply and fishery success; or it may be on a much smaller scale, as in the case of the population explosion of the Crown of Thorns starfish and the subsequent effect of this on the Great Barrier Reef. (See pages 20 and 43 respectively.)

The ocean environment is a dynamic one, continuously changing. Even the very sizes of the oceans are changing. The Atlantic is increasing in size while the Pacific is shrinking. The Red Sea has yet to become an ocean, while the one-time ocean between India and Asia has closed and disappeared, leaving a scar through the Himalayas where the two sides have met.

The physical environment

The structure of the ocean is itself changing, albeit on a timescale almost beyond human comprehension. New sea floor is constantly spreading onto the existing floor, giving rise in certain areas to animal communities that even just a few years ago would have been unimaginable.

At the fringes of the ocean, tons of sediment are being deposited by the world's river systems. These sediments are pouring onto the continental shelves, where different transport processes take over their movement. Massive turbidity currents, for example, carry huge quantities down the continental slopes, carving out submarine canyons as they do so. In contrast, slow, meandering currents flow around the ocean basins – swirling masses of water with particular characteristics of temperature and salinity.

The effects of tides and currents shape the coastlines. The rise and fall of the tides, controlled by the moon and sun, influence the behaviour of animals living on the shores. Waves occur not only at the surface, but also in the ocean depths. These and other forms of turbulence contribute to the circulation of nutrients. The ocean water is a solution of a great variety of chemicals. The distribution of chemicals in the water and sediments is determined by water movement and biological activity.

The chemical environment

Chemicals join the ocean system primarily through erosion of land rocks and transport by river. Once in the ocean, they are incorporated into the deep-ocean sediments or involved in the endless cycles of plant and animal production. Only the hydrothermal vent systems are independent of these cycles, chemicals in this case entering the ocean via a subsurface route.

The constancy of ocean chemistry is more apparent than actual. It is in continuous flux, with chemicals both entering and leaving the system. It seems to be stable and unchanging because of the timescale on which changes occur. Changes are extremely gradual or, if more rapid, are balanced by other changes, so the overall effect is one of stability.

This steady state can be unbalanced by natural events, such as the El Niño phenomenon, and by the actions of man. The unnatural introduction of chemicals into the ocean by man can cause damage either on account of the sheer volume of material involved or because of the chemical complexity of the waste. The effects of such pollution are generally confined to the ocean fringes but can be more widespread.

The biological environment

Interrelationships between marine flora and fauna and the variety of marine habitats can be seen on a number of levels. An example at community level is the sweeping action of kelp fronds. This action keeps surfaces free of debris, thereby enabling the settlement of various fixed species such as sea anemones and sponges. At an individual level there are the worms and shrimps of the hydrothermal vent communities.

Apart from around the vents, the initial production of food is by photosynthesis in the surface layers of the ocean and in the saltmarshes, mangroves and sea grass beds along its fringes. This food is eaten directly by animals – sea cows graze the sea grass, for example, and zooplankton feed on the phytoplankton at the ocean surface. It is also eaten indirectly as it passes along the food chain. When the plants die, their tissues, in the form of raw nutrients, are recycled by currents driven by turbulent action generated by the winds.

Food produced near the surface eventually reaches the ocean floor, either directly as decomposing plant tissue, or indirectly as decomposing animal tissue. There, it is caught up in the chemical cycles and returned to the biological environment by the transport mechanisms of the physical environment.

The vulnerability of the ocean environment is most obvious in the biological sphere, as testified by oiled seabirds, poor catches of fish and so on. Often, by the time damage is apparent the harmful agent has already passed along the chemical pathways and been accumulating in the biological environment for some time. For example, waste metals can dissolve in sea water and enter the food chain

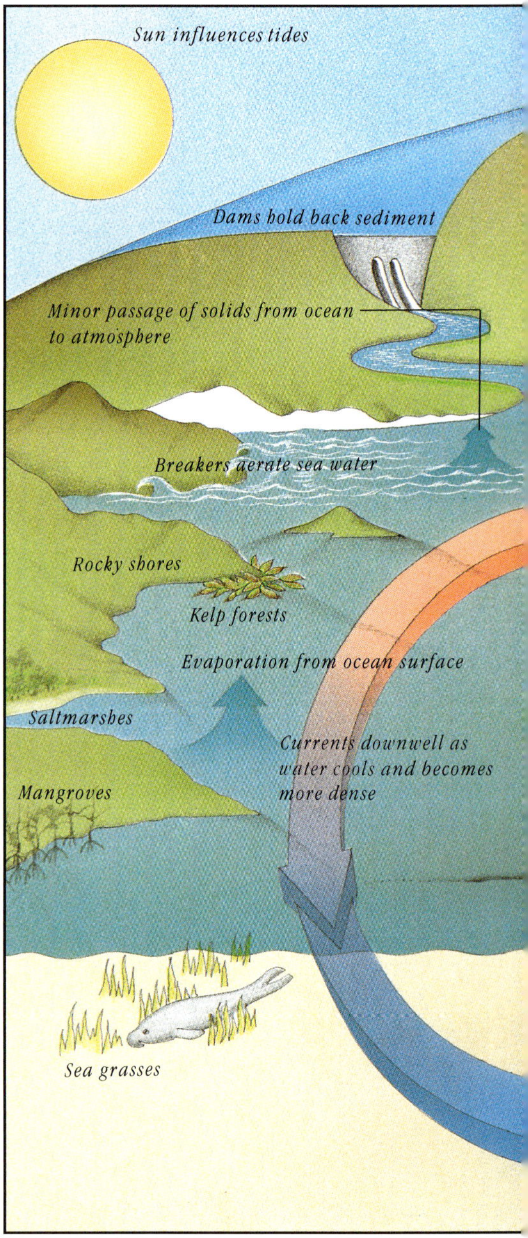

with naturally occurring chemical nutrients. They pass along the chain and can accumulate in certain species of fish. When they reach a certain concentration, they become toxic, and the fish are poisoned and die. It can take even longer for disruption to the physical environment to take visible effect in the biological sphere – such as the damming of a major river and the subsequent prevention of the passage of sediment.

The global environment

As different aspects of the ocean environment interrelate with each other, so the ocean environment as a whole interrelates with the rest of the planet. It does not stand alone. It is coupled to the atmosphere above, to the lithosphere and aesthenosphere below, and to the land around its margins. It is in delicate balance – physically, chemically and biologically.

Below: *This is a schematic representation of some of the processes described in the previous pages. Note how the circulating ocean currents link the biological and chemical parts of the system. Note, too, the relationship between the ocean and the atmosphere above. Clearly in such a complex and delicately balanced arrangement it is difficult to predict the effect of some of man's activities.*

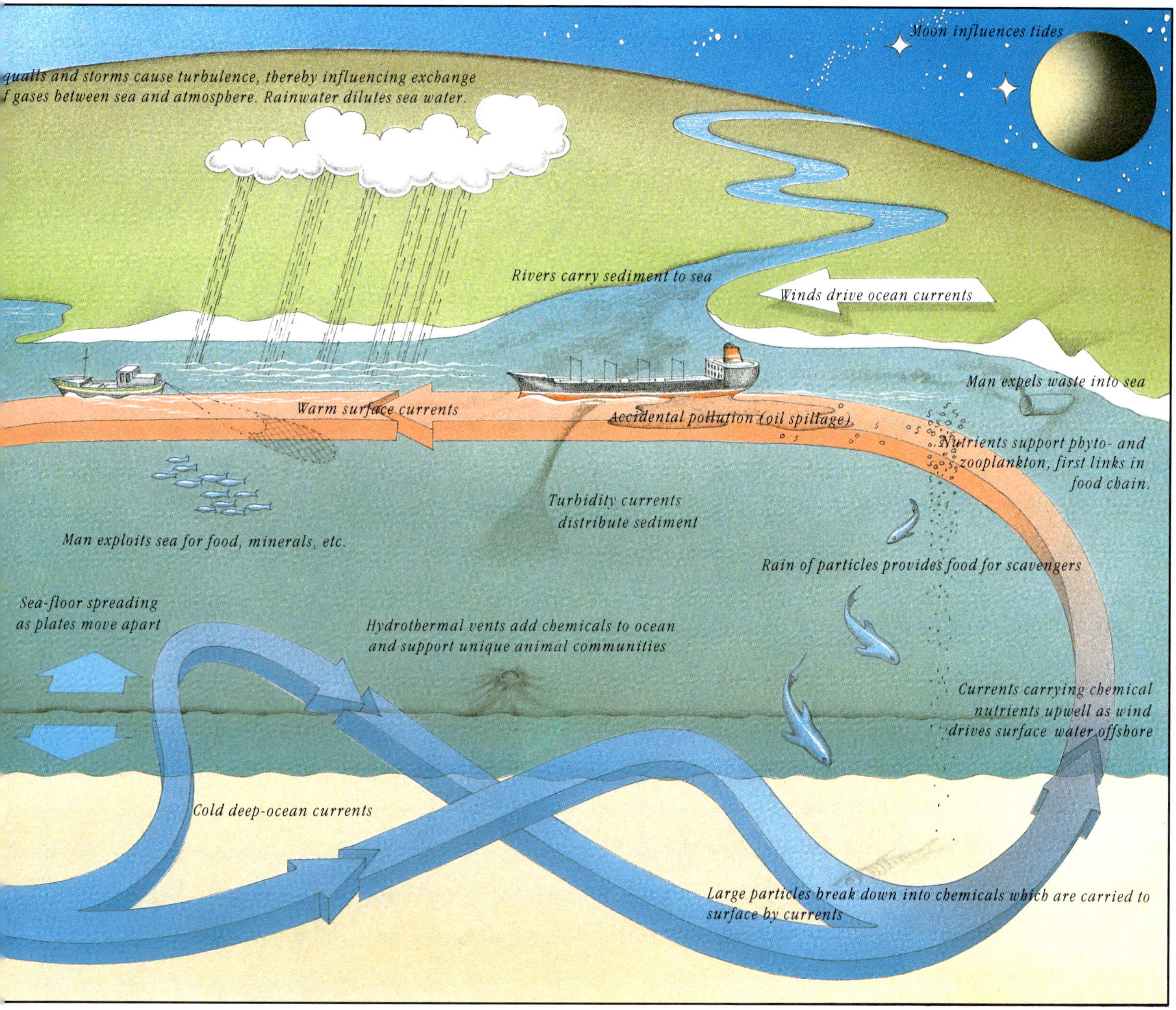

6·RESOURCES FROM THE SEA

OIL

Oil is formed as the result of chemical and biological reactions taking place under seabed sediments. As organic matter, from decomposing animals and plants, is buried under progressively deeper and deeper layers of mud on the bottom of the sea, the pressure from the weight of the overlying sediments increases. This pressure, together with the activity of microorganisms and chemical reactions, results in the formation of hydrocarbons. Oil is a hydrocarbon which occurs as a liquid trapped in rock formations often several thousands of metres under the sea bed. It often has other compounds mixed in with it, such as sulphur, and may vary in consistency from thick tar to almost gas-like compounds.

For oil to accumulate in sufficient quantities to be worthwhile extracting, a number of precise geological conditions must prevail. If the temperature or pressure are too high, the oil will break down further into less complex compounds. It must accumulate in porous rock, such as sandstone or limestone, where it occupies the spaces (pores) between the grains that make up the rock, very much in the way water fills a sponge. Being light, oil tends to rise through the porous rock, so there must be an impervious layer above, such as clay, to trap it.

It costs a great deal to extract oil, particularly from under the sea bed. The water is usually less than 150ft (45m), though sometimes as much as 1000ft (300m), deep. The deeper it is, the more sophisticated is the technology for obtaining the oil in as safe a manner as possible.

Finding oil

Oil may lie a mile or two (2–3km) under the sea bed, yet an oil company must know there is a reasonable chance of finding oil before drilling. Hence it looks for geological formations or structures that allow oil to accumulate, employing geophysicists to map the sea bed and sub-sea features. The information for mapping is provided by a seismic survey.

In a seismic survey, a survey vessel tows a device (airgun) which emits acoustic signals at the sea bed. These penetrate the various layers under the sea bed before being reflected. The depth of their penetration and the nature of their reflection are determined by the composition and structure of the sea bed and sub-sea layers. The reflections are detected by hydrophones, towed as much as 2 miles (3km) behind the vessel. Using the strength of the returning signals and a knowledge of the speed of sound through water, a series of lines (profiles) can be built up, representing a cross-section, or slice, through the rock layers. This picture can be interpreted to identify any potential oil-bearing structures or formations. Today, much of the routine data handling and contouring is carried out by computers able to produce three-dimensional pictures of the sub-sea geology.

Drilling for oil

When a possible oil-bearing formation has been identified, exploratory drilling is carried out to see if oil is present and, if it is, to establish how much there is and what quality it is. Only when satisfied on these points will an oil company begin to produce the oil in commercial quantities. It can be so expensive to reach this stage, particularly as not all exploration sites yield oil or yield it in sufficient quantity, that several companies may join forces. Sometimes a location is not developed until the price of oil is such as to make it worthwhile. For instance, oil in certain small fields in the North Sea would not have been extracted ten years ago because it would have been too expensive.

Once it has been decided to exploit a reservoir, a drilling rig is positioned to sink a series of wells through the sea bed. A platform replaces the rig to complete the drilling and to carry out initial processing of the oil, removing water, sand and other compounds, before pumping it ashore via pipelines.

Wells can take several weeks to drill. To assist the process, a complex liquid (drilling mud) is pumped down to lubricate the drill bit, perhaps thousands of metres beneath the sea bed. It returns to the surface carrying fragments of rock (cuttings). When the oil is ready to flow, it comes up vertical pipes (risers) to the platform, where the hydrocarbons are separated, and pumped ashore or discharged into tankers.

As water begins to leak into the well, it gradually becomes too expensive to separate the oil from it, and new wells may be drilled elsewhere in the field. Production can be enhanced by injecting gas or water under pressure into the reservoir, thereby increasing the upward force. Generally there is insufficient pressure for oil to travel along a pipeline for more than about 9 miles (15km) without being pumped, and impurities which can corrode the inside of the pipe must be removed from the oil. A pipeline is extremely expensive, being made of steel, or an alloy containing chromium or nickel, to reduce corrosion and resist abrasion from sand travelling with the oil.

Right: ***Oil production***
1 *Storage tanks*
2 *Oil refinery*
3 *Pipeline*
4 *Production platform*
5 *Anchor chains*
6 *Impervious layer*
7 *Drill head*
8 *Oil reservoir*
9 *Porous rock*
10 *Oil-bearing rock*

Left: *Geophysicists studying profile data obtained by seismic survey. The different colours represent the layers under the surface of the sea bed. Note the three-dimensional image on the computer screen.*

Oil production

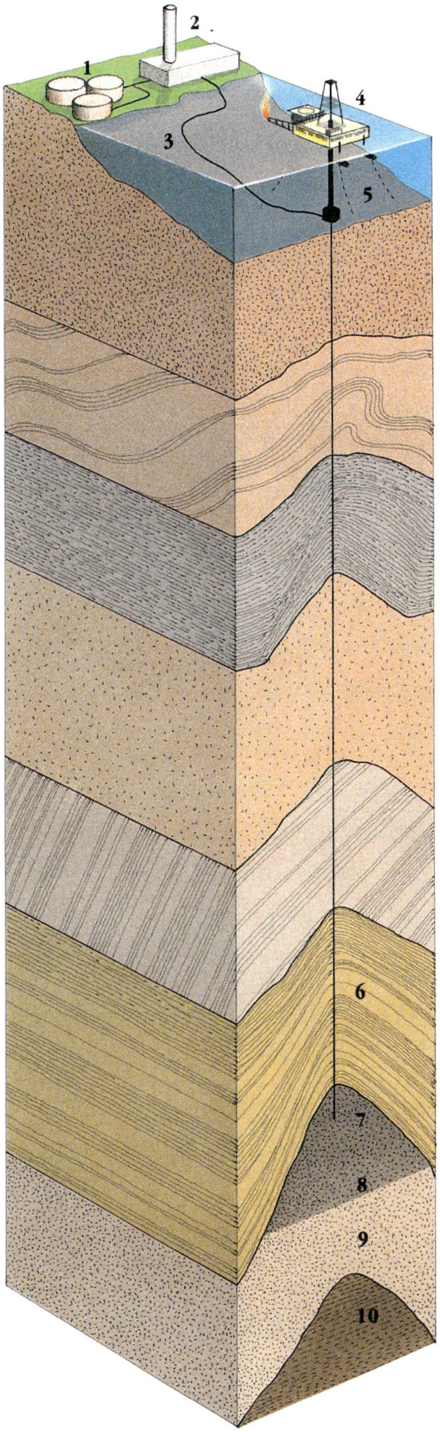

Platforms

A platform is made of steel and concrete and can weigh as much as 650,000 tons. Its hotel-like accommodation and leisure facilities may be home for several hundred workers, men and women, for two or three weeks at a time. It may last for twenty-five years (or sixty, as in the case of one concrete structure) and pump millions of barrels of oil. (A barrel contains 35 gallons, or 160 litres.) It is a hazardous work environment, and all people who work there or visit regularly must undergo thorough survival training, including fire-fighting and emergency drills. The most dangerous areas are off limits to anyone who does not need to be there.

There are about 6000 offshore platforms, and they are even more expensive to remove than to install. When abandoned, they pose a serious navigational hazard to shipping. Current international legislation has not yet been ratified by all oil-producing countries, and even fewer have incorporated the international guidelines into national laws. Some countries insist on complete removal of all platforms, or of smaller ones at least (this is routine in the Gulf of Mexico). Some oil companies want no removal, while others propose to cut old platforms down to a depth of 250ft (75m) below the surface. It has even been suggested to topple them to make them less of a hazard.

One new role for abandoned or cut-down platforms is as artificial reefs for fish.

RICHES FROM THE WATER

For centuries the oceans have been valuable to man as a food source and a highway for transport. With the development of technology, exploitation of sea water – for the energy of its movements and the water itself – is bringing new rewards.

Energy from the sea

Man has long dreamed of harnessing the power of the tides and waves to obtain unlimited and inexpensive energy. While the supply may be unlimited, however, such an operation is certainly not inexpensive in terms of the financial outlay required and of the potential threat to the environment.

Tidal power

The successful harnessing of tidal power requires a rise and fall in the tide each day of at least 16ft (5m). Several sites around the world are under investigation as possibly suitable. To convert the force of the tides into energy, turbines are needed which can be driven by water movement to generate electricity.

To control the water movement, a barrage is constructed across an estuary. The barrage consists of several sections, called caissons, which contain sluices and turbines. The sluices allow the free, uninterrupted passage of water into the area behind the barrage during the flood tide. Additional water can be pumped through the barrage. The sluices are then closed and the falling tide can only escape out of the estuary by passing over the turbines, which spin, generating electricity. There are various operational possibilities for maximising the generation of electricity at any particular stage in this process. Ship locks, fish passes and other features can be incorporated to provide for new, or to maintain existing, uses of the estuary.

Estuaries, because of their funnel shape, often have the required tidal range. However, because of their usefulness as sites for harbours and the development of leisure facilities, not to mention their value in terms of scenic beauty, there is frequently a conflict of interests. The benefits of tidal power have to be balanced with the potential disadvantages to the natural environment.

Wave energy converters

Power transmission unit

Wave energy converter unit housing turbine (red) and power transmission units (green)

Right: *Part of the tidal barrage across La Rance estuary, Brittany, France.*

Wave power

Whereas the harnessing of tidal power is usually confined to estuaries, energy from waves can be obtained along coastal areas. As with tides, waves must be of a considerable size. Another major consideration is that any construction must not be a navigational hazard. Various schemes have been planned and use the same principle of driving a turbine to generate electricity. Like the area behind a tidal barrage, the area immediately behind the row of wave energy converters is quite calm, so any sediment that is suspended in the water is likely to settle out here, which may have implications for the local sea life.

OTEC (Ocean Thermal Energy Conversion)

There is a great difference in temperature between the relatively warm surface waters of the ocean and the cool waters of the deep. In principle, the warm water could be used to evaporate ammonia or propane, which in turn could drive an electricity-generating turbine. The vapourised gas could be reclaimed by condensation, using the cold, deep-ocean water. Such a plant would be extremely large and costly. It would not be economic using today's technology until other sources of energy, particularly fossil fuels, were less abundant and therefore more costly.

Desalination

In very dry countries bordering the sea, and on small islands where there is a lack of fresh water, desalination of sea water is a major means of satisfying the need for large quantities of fresh water. As many as sixty countries obtain their water in this way.

There are several methods by which fresh water may be obtained from sea water. Those in use today include distillation, freezing, ion exchange and osmosis. The local conditions (e.g. availability of power, disposal of waste) and the purposes for which the water itself is required (e.g. drinking, irrigation) determine the process that is used. In many large desalination plants, the heat of the sun is used to distil the water. Where there are nearby oil fields, waste gas can be used to satisfy the energy needs of the plant.

The process of obtaining fresh water from the sea raises the problem of what to do with the salt. This salt is generally in the form of a highly concentrated liquor called brine. The most cost effective way of disposing of this brine is to return it to the sea. However, this must be undertaken most carefully because salt in high concentrations is dangerous to most animals and plants. Brine is much more dense than sea water, so if it was simply pumped back into the sea without special precautions, it would sink and form underwater lakes on the sea bottom. It would mix with the surrounding sea water only very slowly, too slowly not to cause damage to marine life. Consequently, great care must be taken in both the design and positioning of outflow pipes.

Opposite left: *These artist's impressions illustrate how energy from waves is converted into electricity by the driving of a turbine. Because converters like these are moored in coastal waters, they can present a hazard to shipping.*

Right: *A desalination plant in Dubai on the Persian Gulf, United Arab Emirates. Various desalination processes are employed around the world, although in most commercial operations sea water is evaporated to separate it from its salt content and then recondensed.*

FISHING

Catching fish must be one of the earliest ways man had of obtaining food. The kinds of fish that are caught depend on their accessibility and acceptability and also, to some extent, the availability of other types of food. Shrimps, crabs and lobsters are also caught or trapped.

Methods of catching fish

Various methods of catching fish have been developed. Some involve little more than scooping, whereby a net is cast and hauled in. This technique can be employed to catch large numbers of fish, but it can be rather unselective. Fish that are too small to eat may be caught and even if they are returned to the sea, they may be too damaged to survive. Fish that are unpalatable are also caught and suffer a similar fate. Nets can be selective if the mesh is such that only fish of a certain size range are retained. By employing the net in a particular way, too, a certain level of selection can be practised. Unfortunately, even choosing the mesh size cannot help some animals that are caught by accident because they are similar in dimension to the species being sought. Dolphins and porpoises are regularly trapped and die in nets set for tuna fish.

Far more selectivity can be exercised by developing a method that catches only one kind of fish. For example, lines with particular-sized hooks are fairly selective, and the bait used to attract certain species may be unattractive to others.

In general, the fishing technique that is adopted reflects quite closely the level of understanding of the ecology of the fish concerned. For instance, cod tend to swim upwards to escape the mouth of an approaching net, yet are caught because the upper edge of the net overhangs the lower.

Regulation of fishing

As fish stocks are exploited more and more, it becomes increasingly necessary to set limits on what is caught. Size limits are set to ensure that immature fish are not needlessly taken before they have had time to breed. Volume limits are set by governments so that all those who want to catch fish can do so without depleting the stock to the extent that it is unable to sustain itself.

Owing to the intense pressure on the more traditionally sought-after fish, the fishing industry has begun to search very deep water for new varieties. Less is known about the ecology of these deep-water species, so setting limits becomes difficult.

Some countries have started to catch krill, a basic food of some whales. Whales are already under pressure after many years of uncontrolled hunting, and to start taking their food is to add to the problem. Only intense international negotiation curtailed the uncontrolled hunting of some whales. Only time will tell if action was taken soon enough.

Above: *Purse seine nets like this can be many tens of metres in length. A small boat tows one end of the net away from the fishing boat on a long circular route, round a shoal of fish, and eventually back to the fishing boat. Both ends of the net are then drawn in, trapping the fish.*

Left: *A popular fish for farming is the salmon. Here salmon are being returned from the weighing barrel to their pen. Twenty or more cages are tied together in rafts. Walkways between the cages allow farmers to feed the fish, check them for disease or select them for market.*

AQUACULTURE

Aquaculture is the marine equivalent of farming. In many parts of the world aquaculture has been practised for hundreds of years. Freshwater, brackish-water and salt-water fish, together with a number of different types of shellfish such as oysters and mussels, are commonly reared.

Catching fish from the sea requires considerable effort and resources, while rearing them in captivity makes catching them rather more straightforward. Yields can be increased, too, through selective feeding and spacing. Animals which have a sedentary lifestyle, such as oysters and mussels, can be laid on racks or strings in sheltered water in an estuary or inlet and left to grow with relatively little maintenance. Harvesting is then a simple matter of selection and collection.

By its very nature aquaculture entails increasing the productivity of the sea. In other words, it is a way of keeping more individuals within a given area than occurs naturally. The milkfish, which is found in the Far East and is part of the staple diet of certain communities, is a commonly farmed species. In some ponds set aside for the farming of milkfish, 78 tons of fish may be produced per square mile (30 tonnes per sq km), whereas an equivalent area in nearby coastal waters may produce only 17 tons (6.5 tonnes per sq km).

Such concentration of numbers naturally attracts predators, particularly those that normally feed on the species concerned anyway. Much effort has to go into the protection of caged fish. Whereas species such as oysters and mussels do not threaten to escape and, therefore, can simply be laid out to grow, they may need extra precautions to protect them from predators.

Another disadvantage of captive rearing is that if a disease is introduced to the stock, either through the introduction of a diseased individual or in some other way, it can rapidly spread, wiping out the stock or very quickly making it unsaleable.

The curio trade

The curio trade – the collection and sale of marine animals and plants as souvenirs – has developed considerably over recent years, to the extent that it may actually be threatening the survival of certain species or even habitats. A developing awareness of the beauty of the coral reef has brought with it a desire to own a reminder of that beauty. There are regulations to control the trade in many animals but these are often flouted by exporters, importers and shopkeepers.

Harvesting the sea for souvenirs is more akin to fishing than aquaculture. Whereas aquaculture concerns the careful management of resources, collecting souvenirs and fishing are essentially acts of plunder. However, while fishing is now becoming increasingly regulated through the imposition of quotas, the collection of souvenirs remains virtually unregulated. This situation is changing only gradually as certain species are brought under the protection of international legislation. (See Chapter 7.)

7 · Management of the Sea

THREATS

Man's use of the sea has increased through the ages, particularly during the last century. It has now become a threat to the natural balance of the marine ecosystem. Species, habitats and whole seas are endangered, most commonly by man's quest for food, his disposal of waste, and coastal development.

Food from the sea

Although man's food from the sea includes the meat of whales, seals, porpoises and turtles, as well as shellfish and seaweed, the main food item is, of course, fish. More than a quarter of fish caught, however, is not eaten directly. Instead, it is converted into oil, animal foodstuffs or fertilizer.

During the last few years, the annual world catch of fish has been increasing only slowly and has not kept up with growing demand. Fish catches are often regulated on the basis of 'maximum sustainable yield', meaning as many fish may be caught as can be replaced naturally by the remaining fish population. A situation in which too many fish are caught and the population begins to decline is known simply as 'overfishing'.

The maximum sustainable yield for a particular species in a given part of the ocean is extremely difficult to estimate, because of the wide variety of natural processes that determine fish mortality. As important as the numbers of fish caught is their size. If too many small fish are caught, even after they have spawned (reproduced), the average size of fish in the population is eventually reduced. This is called 'growth overfishing'. On the other hand, if fish are caught that have not yet reproduced, the number of fish being added to the population declines and the population therefore shrinks. This is called 'recruitment overfishing'.

Sometimes the reaction to overfishing is to increase the mesh size of nets in order to save local livelihoods, but this is not always to the good of the fishery in the long term.

The hunting of the blue whale provides a classic example of mismanagement. Even though it was known blue whales were becoming fewer in the early 1930s, they were still being caught in similar numbers through increased effort in the early 1960s. Soon, however, no amount of extra effort could secure the required catches. The remaining blue whales were too few and too young to breed; as a result, the population was simply disappearing.

The blue whale was just the first of many whale species to be hunted until there were too few to make it worthwhile. As its decline became rapid, krill – the small, shrimp-like crustaceans on which it feeds – underwent a population explosion. Their main predator no longer existed in numbers adequate to crop them. Whalers turned to krill as an alternative catch, but since the early 1980s, volumes caught have been halving each year...

Waste

Almost any unwanted substance finds its way into the sea eventually, from plastics to petroleum, pesticides to nuclear waste, sewage to metals. In general, waste accumulates at the ocean fringe where it is discharged or dumped. There are exceptions, however: oil tanker spills and floating garbage may be carried a long way.

Waste disposal threatens habitats rather than species directly. Most endangered are semi-enclosed areas, such as estuaries and seas like the Mediterranean.

Different substances do damage in different ways. Some are toxic: tributyl tin, a substance in paint applied to the hull of many yachts and ships, is an example. Others have a smothering effect, such as waste fibre from paper pulp mills. Yet others, being organic, are broken down by bacteria, a process which depletes the water of oxygen.

Coastal development

A major development is the reclaiming of land from the sea. As much as 18 per cent of the Netherlands consists of reclaimed land. Estuaries, being ideal areas for reclamation, are particularly threatened. The new land is commonly used for the siting of housing, petrochemical plants, and sea- and airports.

Other developments include the building of power and desalination plants. Power stations use water from the sea for cooling. When this is returned, it is warmer than the surrounding sea. Desalination plants return water much more highly concentrated in salt than ordinary sea water. The foraging and nursery ground areas of many animals, such as shrimps, are often threatened by such discharges. They tend to be shallow and not readily flushed by the sea, hence harmful agents remain undispersed.

Further damage to coastal habitats is caused by the construction of tidal barrages, marinas and other amenities.

Right: *This is a Landsat image of Holland showing Amsterdam and the IJsselmeer, a huge area of sea being gradually reclaimed as land. The image has been coloured by computer and does not depict actual colours. Just outside the entrance to the IJsselmeer are the West Friesian Islands. A dyke has been built across the entrance (seen as a white line). Behind the dyke substantial tracts of land, known as polders, have been reclaimed. Note the distinctive blue patterns of the polder fields. A second phase of reclamation is planned behind the dyke dividing off the lower end of the IJsselmeer. Amsterdam is the blue-green area to the left at the bottom of this section.*

Left: Euphasia superba, *the Antarctic krill which is a principal part of the diet of baleen whales (such as the blue whale). In the early 1980s, fishing fleets from West Germany, Poland, Russia, Japan and Taiwan harvested the vast shoals of krill, taking some 20,000 tonnes annually. The fleets used sonar to detect the shoals then tracked them with satellites. The imposing of catch quotas has been suggested as a means of preventing over-exploitation.*

WASTE DISPOSAL

The discarding of unwanted materials into coastal seas may have been appropriate when centres of population were small and waste was non-toxic and easily broken down. Since the two world wars, however, populations have swollen and waste products have grown in volume and chemical complexity. It can no longer be assumed that the sea can simply absorb whatever is put in it.

Waste may enter the sea directly through specially sited outlets, or indirectly after being discharged into rivers and streams. Some is dumped from ships, some in licensed areas. Even rain can carry pollutants.

Some pollution is accidental – an oil spill, for example. Certain waste is 'degradable', i.e. it breaks down into less complex, harmless substances. Examples include domestic effluent, agricultural waste, by-products of food and drink processing, paper pulp waste, and certain chemical and oil waste. Other pollutants lose their harmful character as they are diluted by the sea, such as the warm water expelled from power stations and some acids. Yet other waste occurs as particles, e.g. dredging spoil, ash, colliery waste, clays and various plastics. Some discarded material remains chemically active for a long time, including metals, chlorinated pesticides and radioactive waste.

Different kinds of waste are not necessarily discharged in isolation. It may be straightforward to predict the impact on the environment of one type of waste, but not of waste 'cocktails'.

Right: *A beach on the coast of Brittany, France, being cleaned up after an oil spill. If a slick is reached before it grounds, and if the sea is not too rough, it can be contained within booms and the oil skimmed off into barges. Alternatively, chemicals can be applied to break up the oil into small particles which sink or disperse. Nowadays, however, this method is considered undesirable, since the chemicals can be toxic to marine life. Once a slick has come ashore, contaminated sand or shingle is removed and rocks are jet washed. Marine fauna and flora can take many years to recover from such a damaging event.*

Domestic effluent

Discharging domestic effluent raises two problems. First, there is the threat of disease. Bacteria in sewage, for example, are a danger to those who swim, waterski, surf, etc. in the sea and may swallow polluted water. Second, discharges of nitrates and phosphate can over-enrich the sea water in nutrients and bring about the excessive proliferation of algae. 'Algal blooms' of this kind, which may be visible over wide areas of the sea's surface, can be toxic to fish and other marine life.

Left: *The outlet of a sewage outfall pipe. The effluent is buoyant and rises towards the surface of the sea. Siting outlets under water thus allows a longer period of dilution and more effective dispersal of the waste than siting them above the surface.*

Below: *Contamination of a beach arising from the extraction of titanium dioxide. The red stain in the foreground is from the iron salts left over after the process of extraction from the parent ore.*

Industrial waste

Many people assume the sea can simply dilute waste and thus render it harmless. This is to ignore, however, the complex, interlinking roles of sediments, plants and animals in the passage of chemicals through the ocean. Many forms of marine life actually concentrate waste substances as these are passed along a food chain, sometimes to the extent that the substances become toxic. This commonly happens to metals. More dangerous, however, are synthetic compounds. As these do not occur in nature, the natural breakdown mechanisms of the marine environment cannot always cope with them.

Thermal waste

Cold sea water is used by power stations for cooling. It becomes warm during the cooling process and is then returned to the sea. This thermal waste water can increase substantially the local temperature of the sea. Most organisms can survive within only narrow temperature ranges and are therefore at risk. The sea temperature falls rapidly, however, with increasing distance from the point of discharge. Warm water of this kind can be used in fish rearing.

Air pollution

Gypsum (calcium sulphate) and pulverised fuel ash (PVA) are by-products of the process which reduces the emission of sulphur dioxide from coal-fired power stations. In one scheme, these by-products are mixed with cement (rather than stockpiled) to make blocks, which are used to construct artificial reefs on the sea bed for colonisation by marine life, especially fish and shellfish, which can then be harvested.

Problems of management

One of the main problems in waste management is demonstrating clearly the processes of cause and effect after a discharge of waste. This can take a long time, and environmental deterioration may be advanced by the time legislation is introduced to prevent further discharges of a similar kind. The release of chlorofluorocarbons, which destroy the ozone layer, and sulphur dioxide, a primary ingredient of acid rain, have been observed by scientists for many years. Likewise the burning of much primary forest, which lessens the uptake of carbon dioxide from the atmosphere and thus contributes to the greenhouse effect. It is only in the last two or three years, however, that governments have taken any action.

LEGISLATION

The immense size of the oceans makes them, in the eyes of many, a most convenient dustbin. It also makes the monitoring of waste disposal particularly difficult. Further problems centre on the question of ownership of the oceans.

Ownership of the oceans

Through the centuries, countries with a coastline have claimed certain rights over 'their' sea. Out of these 'historical' rights have grown various international understandings of what can be accepted as a reasonable claim.

A coastal nation lays claim to 'territorial waters', which extend a variable distance from its coastline, usually between three and twelve nautical miles. Further offshore it has 'exclusive economic zones' (EEZs), extending some 200 nautical miles out to sea. The purpose of EEZs is to define boundaries within which the nation claiming them enjoys certain rights in international law. These rights concern exploitation of mineral and fisheries resources within the zones. Beyond the EEZs are 'international waters' (the high seas). It is extremely difficult to fix all these various limits.

Protecting the ocean margins

Apart from transport and military activities, most uses of the sea (e.g. waste disposal, fishing, mining) tend to be restricted to its margins. It is these uses that individual countries are able to influence, by setting environmental standards and making laws to enforce them. Many countries have such standards and laws, but have met with varying degrees of success in applying them. Regulation is particularly difficult when conflicts of interest arise, either between member states of a federal nation (e.g. the USA), or between countries on the same continental mass which, for example, have the same river flowing through them (e.g. Europe).

In order that certain species or habitats are protected, international cooperation is required. For instance, trading in many species of coral and shellfish has been restricted since 1985, when they came under CITES – the Convention on International

Above: *In many places around the world, reefs such as these have been plundered for their coral (for display or building purposes), their fish (for home aquaria) and for other creatures. Marine reserves can reduce pressure on vulnerable ecosystems of this kind.*

Right: *This clam is found around the Maldive Islands and is a protected species. Unregulated collecting makes legal protection vital if the natural heritage of coral islands is to remain and to be enjoyed by future generations of both islanders and tourists.*

Right: *A satellite view of the Mediterranean Sea. This sea is bordered by many countries with different politics and cultures. A diversity of interests is inevitable, making it difficult to reach agreement on how to proceed in coping with pan-national pollution.*

Trade in Endangered Species. Some countries, including the Philippines, imposed a complete ban on exports of raw coral and giant clams in 1987.

In some cases there is no immediate threat but measures are needed to prevent further damage from coastal development. Some countries create marine reserves or parks, recognised by law, where species and habitats can remain undisturbed. There are a number of these around the USA and Australia. Elsewhere legal protection is too difficult to enforce and voluntary measures are encouraged.

More ambitious are those countries co-operating in an attempt to protect whole areas of sea under threat. Many countries have signed the Oslo and Paris Conventions, which offer some protection to the North Sea and north-east Atlantic Ocean. Such agreements take many years to formulate, because of differences in national self-interest, political will, culture and available funds. The Mediterranean Action Plan, set up by the United Nations Environment Programme in 1975, is a major project designed to assist countries with conflicting interests to co-operate in protecting the Mediterranean. This sea is threatened by pollution, shipping and fishing development, and oil and mineral exploitation. The plan has become a prototype for others in coastal areas around parts of South America, the Caribbean, West Africa and South-East Asia.

Protecting the whole ocean

Given the necessary financial and human resources and the political will, protection of the ocean margin is a practical proposition. Protection of the ocean as a whole is much more of a problem – scientifically, economically and politically. A number of conventions, protocols and international understandings seek to address the problems of the ocean environment as a whole; these problems, however, are not themselves well understood. That they exist, or are likely to do so soon, is understood. How serious they will become and what the full implications are for the future remains uncertain. Consequently, it is difficult to decide upon and implement appropriate remedial action.

THINGS TO DO

There are a lot of things you can do after reading this book if you wish to pursue further your interest in the undersea world.

Museums

You could visit a museum which has a section on the sea. There is a museum in nearly every major town. It may cover local interests or have a particular theme, such as geology or natural history. Your local library or information centre will probably have details of museums near you, and be able to tell you about any special events or exhibitions due to take place at them in the near future.

Sealife centres

These are becoming very popular and are to be found in many holiday resorts. They aim to show their exhibits in as natural a state as possible and generally focus on the marine life that is found locally. They often feature 'touch tanks' with animals visitors can pick up and hold, such as starfish and crabs.

Books

All major booksellers have a range of books on wildlife of the seas and oceans. Technical books which cover in greater depth all aspects of the undersea world outlined in this book are generally obtainable from more specialised bookshops, or specialised departments within particularly large bookshops. Shops of this kind are usually found in towns with centres of higher education, such as universities and polytechnics. In addition, your local library should have a selection of relevant books and be able to order any specific title for you to borrow.

Organisations

In most countries, there are a number of scientific organisations, such as marine research institutes, which deal with oceanographic subjects. Some of these organisations concentrate on specialised areas while others have a more general concern. Your local museum or university should be able to direct you to a body appropriate to your particular interest. Some organisations exercise restricted membership and are generally only for those with qualifications in some relevant subject, but they can be a fruitful source of information.

There is a growing number of organisations concerned particularly about damage to the natural environment, including the oceans, and which campaign regularly over problems in general or over specific issues. Membership of these is open to the general public, and they provide plenty of opportunity for those who wish to become involved in a practical way in the protection of the sea. These organisations frequently advertise in newspapers or natural history magazines.

Courses

There are many courses for those who wish to pursue their interest in a formal manner. Some courses assume a certain level of knowledge and can lead to a qualification of some kind. Others assume no prior knowledge and lead either to a qualification or

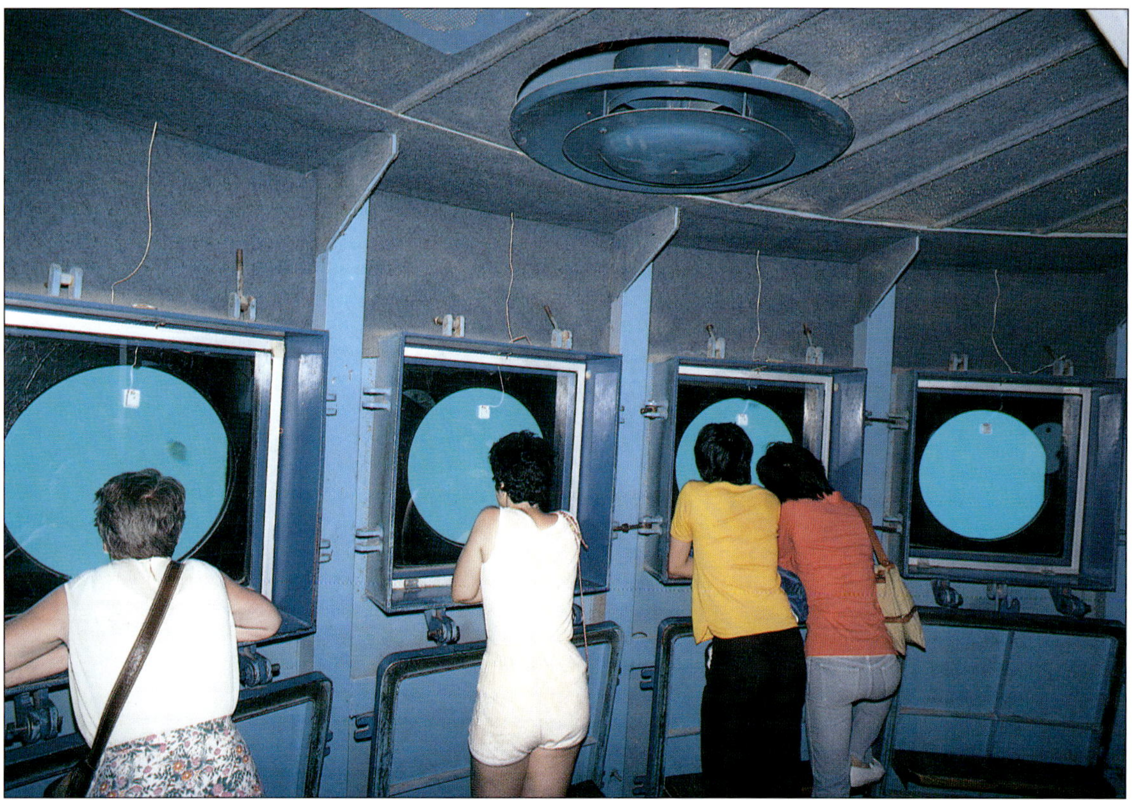

Left: *Underwater observation chambers open to the public can be found around the world, particularly in tropical or subtropical countries. From these chambers it is possible to enjoy the spectacle of fish feeding (food is often dropped into the water on purpose to attract fish in large numbers) and to feast one's eyes on corals, giant clams, sea slugs, sting rays and other living wonders of the undersea world.*

Right: *Snorkeling is the most accessible means of experiencing the marine world at first hand. A simple waterproof camera can be used to record its magic.*

are purely of recreational interest. Some courses, particularly the recreational kind, are residential and include a lot of practical work and excursions. Details of courses are generally available at major libraries.

Visits to the sea

There is no better way to understand the sea and its mysteries than to visit it. You can walk along the tideline or the water's edge, explore rock pools, examine the sand or shingle, and even go into the sea itself. A magnifying lens and a handbook on the seashore are invaluable and enable you to get far more out of your visit. Binoculars are useful for observing birdlife, particularly if the shore is a mudflat and the tide recedes a long way. As the tide falls, many different species of bird can be seen probing, pecking and dabbling in the exposed mud.

Remember the Seashore Code for Conservation:

- Watch shorelife without disturbing it.
- If you do disturb any shorelife, return it to its place.
- Put back turned rocks and stones in their original position.
- Do not pull seaweed off the rocks.
- Do not disturb feeding and nesting birds.
- Take all your litter home.

To experience the sea more fully you have to swim in it, either with a snorkel and mask or with scuba diving equipment. Snorkeling on a warm day over a rocky shore at high tide, when the rock pools are covered, can be magical. However, it is essential that you have the right gear and are a good swimmer. Swimming pools often run short courses which enable you to learn all that is necessary to snorkel safely and with confidence.

After learning to snorkel, the next step is to venture underwater using SCUBA – Self-Contained Underwater Breathing Apparatus. This enables you to swim well below the surface and to explore further afield. Again, courses for learning how to scuba dive are available at many swimming pools. Ask at your local pool for details.

- Remember: NEVER SNORKEL OR DIVE ON YOUR OWN.

GLOSSARY

A

Abyssal plain
The vast expanse of flat sea floor which stretches between an ocean ridge and a continental slope or ocean trench.
Acid rain
Rain which is a solution of sulphur dioxide and therefore acidic. It can damage vegetation (including woodland), lakes and buildings.
Aesthenosphere
The layer of the earth which underlies the lithosphere. It is the outer section of a much thicker layer called the mantle, the whole of which is molten.
Asdic
Allied Submarine Detection Investigation Committee.
Atoll
A ring-shaped coral reef.

C

Constructive margin
The site along which sea-floor spreading is taking place as a result of two plates moving apart. Also, a continental margin along which the continent and ocean basin are on the same plate.
Continental margin
The site along which a continental mass and an ocean basin meet.
Continental rise
The gentle gradient at the very foot of the continental slope.
Continental shelf
The gently sloping sea bed which borders a continent.
Continental slope
The steep slope from the continental shelf down to the continental rise and the abyssal plain.
Crust
The crust is the surface layer of the earth. It is the outer layer of the lithosphere.

D

Deep-ocean floor
The area that lies between the foot of a continental slope and an ocean ridge. Abyssal plains and ocean trenches both fall within the province of the deep-ocean floor.
Destructive margin
The site along which two plates are colliding and one is being forced, or subducted, under the other. One plate can be continental and the other oceanic, or both plates can be oceanic.
Dilute
To reduce the concentration of a solution by adding more liquid.
Downwelling
Flowing downwards.

E

Ecosystem
The interaction between a community of interdependent organisms and the environment they inhabit.
Element
A chemical substance which cannot be broken down into a simpler form.
Erosion
The wearing away of the land surface by natural forces.
Estuary
The mouth of a river where the tide enters.
Evaporation
The loss of liquid, in the form of vapour, to the atmosphere as a result of the latter being warmer than the former.

F

Fishery
The natural occurrence of large numbers of fish and the catching of these by Man.
Food chain
A series of plants and animals each of which is eaten by the next in the series.

G

Global warming
The warming up of the world's atmosphere resulting from the accumulation within it of certain gases which are trapping the sun's heat. Commonly known as the greenhouse effect.
Greenhouse effect
See **Global warming.**
Groundwater
Water found in the surface soil on land.

H

Hydrocarbon
A substance which is organic in origin and consists only of hydrogen and carbon.
Hydrothermal activity
The heating and movement of water associated with the presence of hot- and warm water vents along the site of sea-floor spreading.

I

Inorganic
Inorganic material is mineral in origin and does not come from animals or plants.

L

Land uplift
The raising of land caused by geological movement.
Lithosphere
The outermost layer of the earth; itself divided into the outer lithosphere, or crust, and the inner lithosphere.
Lunar cycle
The repeated orbiting of the moon round the earth.

M

Magma
The molten rock of the mantle.
Mantle
The thick layer of molten rock under the lithosphere. Its outer section is called the aesthenosphere.
Mid-ocean ridge
See **Ocean ridge.**
Mudflat
An expanse of muddy shore exposed at low tide.

N

Nitrate
A chemical which serves as an important nutrient, or food, for phytoplankton.
Nutrient
A substance which provides nourishment. The chemicals nitrate and phosphate are the principal nutrients, or food, of phytoplankton.
Nutrient regeneration
The process by which dead animals and plants decay and undergo chemical breakdown, and the chemicals so released serve once more as nutrients for phytoplankton.

O

Ocean margin
The edge of the ocean. Usually defined as extending no further than the continental shelf.
Ocean plain
See **Abyssal plain.**
Ocean ridge
A ridge on the ocean floor formed of magma which has upwelled between two plates that are pulling apart.
Ocean(ic) trench
A trench or valley formed at the foot of a continental slope where two plates are colliding and one is being forced, or subducted, under the other.
Organic
Organic material comes from animals or plants. It is not mineral in origin.

Ozone layer
A layer in the upper atmosphere of a particular form of oxygen, produced by the interaction of ordinary oxygen with ultraviolet rays from the sun. By absorbing these rays, the ozone layer protects the earth from excessive and damaging ultraviolet radiation.

P

Phosphate
A chemical which serves as an important nutrient, or food, for phytoplankton.
Photosynthesis
The process by which plants grow as they convert carbon dioxide into tissue under the influence of sunlight. Also important to the process are suitable nutrients and the green pigment chlorophyll.
Phytoplankton
The forms of microscopic plant life that float and drift in the sea.
Plate
Plates (or more precisely, tectonic plates) are the moving sections which make up the earth's outer layer, the lithosphere. On the surface of the plates are the continents and oceans.
Pollution
The introduction of man-made products, often waste, into the natural environment. More generally, any destruction by Man of the environment, such as that caused by land reclamation and building.
Productivity
Reproduction and growth. **Plankton p.** – reproduction and growth of plankton. **Biological p.** – reproduction and growth of living things generally.

S

Saline
Salty.
Salinity
Saltiness.
Sea-floor spreading
The formation of new sea floor where two plates are pulling apart. Magma from the mantle upwells between the plates and attaches to them as it solidifies.
Solution
A mixture of liquid and solid material, liquid and gas, or all three. The solid material has been dissolved in the liquid, and the gas chemically combined with it.
Steady state
Describes the constant nature of a system as a result of substances leaving and entering it in equal quantity. The ocean as a whole is described as being in a chemical steady state, the overall quantity and concentration of chemicals in it never changing.

Subduction
The forcing of one plate under another, and its incorporation into the mantle, where two plates are colliding.
Subsidence
The lowering of land caused by geological movement.
Suspension
A mixture of liquid and solid particles. The particles are said to be suspended in the liquid, i.e. not dissolved.

T

Thermocline
In the ocean, that section of the water column through which the temperature rapidly falls on moving from the warmer surface waters to the cooler deep waters.
Turbidity current
A sediment-laden flow which runs down the continental slope. It is denser than unladen sea water.
Turbulence
Disturbance, sometimes violent, within a body of water or gas.

U

Uplift(ing)
See **Land uplift.**
Upwelling
Flowing upwards.

W

Water column
A body of water perceived in the vertical.
Water table
The level below which the ground is saturated with water.
Weathering
Wearing caused by the passage of water or wind.

Z

Zooplankton
The forms of microscopic animal life that drift or float in the sea.

INDEX

Page references set in *italic* type refer to subjects mentioned in illustration captions.

Picture Credits

Photographs are credited by page number and by their position on the page, as follows: (T) Top; (B) Bottom; (R) Right; (L) Left; FC Front Cover; BC Back Cover.

Energy Technology Support Unit: 50(T)
Institute of Oceanographic Sciences, Deacon Laboratory: 9(L), 15(B)
Planet Earth Pictures: Pete Atkinson 17(T); Peri & April Coelho 31; Leo Collier 42–3(B); Peter Capen 52(B); Peter David 1, 44; Walter Deas 38; Georgette Douwma 23; J. Duncan 52(T); Robert Hessler 11(T), 27(L); F. Jack Jackson 28(B); Joyce Photographics 41(T); Robert A. Jureit 30; James King 27(R); Kenneth Lucas 20(T), 45(T); John Lythgoe F&BC, 3, 19, 39(L), 40, 60; C. Maddock 51; Larry Madin 4; Bora Merdsoy 54; NASA/Flip Schulke 17(B); 63; Carl Roessler 43(R); Keith Scholey 20–21(B); Flip Schulke FC(R), 12(B), 58(T), 61; Peter Scoones FC(L), 6–7, 22(T), 22(B); Herwarth Voigtmann 18, 58(B); Alex Williams 15(T); Warren Williams 39(R), 53, 57(T); Bill Wood 28(T), 42–3(T); Norbert Wu 41(B)
RIDA Photo Library: David Bayliss 37(L)
Salamander Books Ltd: 33
Science Photo Library: Aerospace Corporation 34–5(B); Earth Satellite Corporation 55; Bob Edwards 57(B); European Space Agency 59; Dr George Gornacz 45(B); Jan Hinsch 24, 29; Institute of Oceanographic Sciences 9(R); Berretty Rapho 56; Peter Ryan 37; Peter Ryan/Scripps Institution of Oceanography, University of California 26
Shell Photographic Library: 48, 49(R)
Spectrum Colour Library: 50(B)